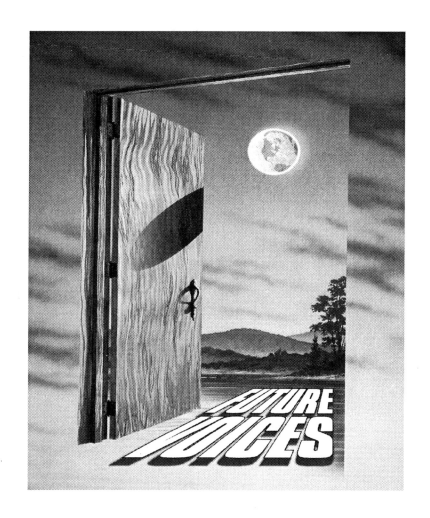

FROM SOUTH WEST ENGLAND

Edited by Carl Golder

First published in Great Britain in 2000 by
YOUNG WRITERS
Remus House,
Coltsfoot Drive,
Woodston,
Peterborough, PE2 9JX
Telephone (01733) 890066

HB ISBN 0 75431 862 1
SB ISBN 0 75431 863 X

FOREWORD

This year, the Young Writers' Future Voices competition proudly presents a showcase of the best poetic talent from over 42,000 up-and-coming writers nationwide.

Successful in continuing our aim of promoting writing and creativity in children, our regional anthologies give a vivid insight into the thoughts, emotions and experiences of today's younger generation, displaying their inventive writing in its originality.

The thought, effort, imagination and hard work put into each poem impressed us all and again the task of editing proved challenging due to the quality of entries received, but was nevertheless enjoyable. We hope you are as pleased as we are with the final selection and that you continue to enjoy *Future Voices From South West England* for many years to come.

CONTENTS

The Poems

WHY?

I'm sat here deep in thought
About what my gran has just said
She told me about when she was 12
And the air was clean instead
She told us about the thousands of stars
And she said that the sky was light blue
But now it is a hazy pink
And the sun is always burning too.
Back then, she said there were smaller seas
And ice caps which have now gone
There were animals called penguins and polar bears
Which now are all long gone
In the winter soft flakes of white ice
Would gently fall from the sky
It was called snow and they played in it
But I've never seen it, why?
When she was a child they played outside
Chasing each other with glee
But surely that can't be any better
Than computer games or TV
I did think my generation was cool
And technology was really great
But life in 2073
Has a side that I really hate!

Lucy Bence-Wilkins (12)

THE SIXTH YEAR DOLL

Her screaming voice was angry,
High pitched screeching brakes forced to halt
Abruptly.

Unwilling tyres, locked, still.
Piercing smell of scoured rubber,
Diffused into a neat ball of smoke around her powerful frame.

Reality came slow.
I watched as if an outsider, her
Unforgiving smooth curve,
Tossed her casually, as if she was a neglected doll,
Thrown into oblivion and drifting down again.
She hangs in the air gracefully . . .

Head first.
Slap . . . crack, bang back down in front,
(Like the owner's hand, grasping the small waist of the doll firmly
And then her body driven into the concrete - squashed like an insect)
Landing on an uncomfortable patch,
Far from the mark . . .

Head back and tucked under.
No cry, no tear, in a disfigured heap,
Motionless she sighs,
Calm and peaceful. Her eyes are wide
And still sparkling.

Looking over her golden bloody locks
Covered a half broken badge,
'Six Today!'

Maisey Wong (16)

FALLOUT

A world full of terror and pain
Lies awaiting for more corpses to fall
Onto its dormant floor
People die, falling like terrified dominoes
As radiation takes over their bodies
Children left in corners weep till
Pools of water form beneath their shivering feet
Their minds filled with explosions and screams
From innocent children lost in their own homes
Some being embraced by the power of death
Others pale, captured by the strength of no hope.
It's all over the world goes black
No sound, silence, silence, silence
As the radiation wipes over the world
No humans, no life.

Georgina Prichard (13)
Badminton School

A LIFE GONE

The break of dawn
An early bird sings
Upon the sound of beating wings
A flower blooms
The day passes
Again, the bird sings
The flower closes
All is still,
Dead
Until the morning,
Waiting, for the break of dawn.

Celia Jones (12)
Badminton School

A GIRL'S HEAD

A girl's head is full of ambition,
hope and thought for the future.
Yet at the same time,
a head which has questions of, 'How do I get out of
my music lesson?'
With answers of excuses of these matters.

A head full of laughter,
happiness, joy and a smile.
Until told to do work and then a head full of misery,
sadness and disappointment.

It's a head which thinks of responsibility
and how and what they will be when they are older.
A head which looks forward to the good things in life
and dreads the bad.

Whatever is in a girl's head is something that nobody
other than she herself can explain.

Lara Strang (13)
Badminton School

MYSELF

Hello, my name is Rebecca Louise Brothers
And in my life I've had no others.
They say my hair is sparkly brown,
But I think it is gold, like a crown.
My eyes are blue, some say they're green;
My nose, part of my face, is in-between.
Lanky legged? Yes, it's me -
And there is no other I'd prefer to be.

Rebecca Brothers (12)
Badminton School

4

IF . . .

If Kennedy wasn't assassinated,
What would happen, I wonder,
Would the world blow up?
The question I often ponder.
The answer came from the telly,
It hit me in the face,
What would happen if you had a machine,
Taking you to any time and any place.
The crew of the ship needed curry
It was a Red Dwarf sitcom
They tried the machine to get it
But this trip went horribly wrong.
They ended up stopping the killing,
Which was a big mistake.
The Russians won the space race
And part of the US was a lake.
The Cubans were nuclear warlords,
They had America under threat.
Lister ate a dead man,
He did this for a bet.
It ended up OK
Kennedy killed himself.
He was the man round the grassy knoll
So the US got lots of wealth.
Would this happen if Kennedy wasn't killed?
That's what most people would wonder.
The world won't blow up, I now know;
This question I will no longer ponder.

Cordelia Witton (12)
Badminton School

DREAM

I was but a dream,
I floated in the midnight hour,
Through windows bewitched by romance,
Looking for the right mind into which to insert myself.
I was but a dream.

I was but an idea,
I was pondered over,
I was debated,
I was suggested.
I was but an idea.

The dream became an idea,
The idea became a certainty,
The certainty became a thing,
The dream was developed,
The idea was developed,
The certainty was developed.

The thing was different,
It was brought into the world and developed there.

Frances Richardson (12)
Badminton School

THE FUTURE

I wonder what the future holds
For you, for me, as it unfolds.
I must be bold and stand up tall,
And make a difference to us all.

My greatest fear is nuclear war,
For the hungry, the homeless, the sick and the poor.
Ours are the voices of things to come,
Tomorrow, next month and the millennium.

We must make a difference, work as one,
Ban the bomb, the knife and the gun.
Feed the hungry, help the poor,
House the homeless one and all.

The richer folk must help the poor,
Go without and give much more.
A little less for you and me,
Would help the world, just wait and see.

Kathryn Bath (12)
Badminton School

A GIRL'S HEAD

In it there is a house for dolls
There is a garden full of flowers.

There are cute little bunny rabbits
And big colourful lollipops.

There are plastic pots for cooking
Tea for your toys
And there are long, pretty dresses.

There are dreams of being pretty
To attract all the gents,
Dreams of being older and knowing how to fly.

There are places for shopping with friends
And excuses for not swimming.

There are questions such as when do lessons finish
And why there are exams?

A girl's head is a box full of surprises.

Javian Tang (14)
Badminton School

FOOD

I love food so much,
I just can't get enough,
I eat it slow,
I eat it fast,
I've never tried to make it last.

I don't like tomatoes,
But I do like potatoes,
Chocolate is the nicest,
I'd never dare to waste it.

Why is it that,
The only things I like are bad for me?
It's my mum that tells me off,
But I still love food so much!

Anna C Westropp (13)
Badminton School

I WISH

I wish I'd brushed my hair last night,
I wish it were brown not white.

I wish I had some really cool clothes,
Like bell bottoms, hipsters and all those.

I wish I didn't have a brace,
I look such a disgrace.

I wish I was good at work,
And had a good degree

And I wish I had a hammer
To smash the mirror into space.

Jessica Williams (11)
Badminton School

VOICES THAT INFLUENCE

You have twenty-five seconds in which to decide . . .
Which detergent is softer.
It'll give you wrinkle-free skin . . .
And is only half-price!

It only lasts till the end of the month!
Should you hide, or go and fight?
We need your help,
It's the latest in fashion and style!

Does my bum look too big in this?
Roast lunch, just like Mum cooked it,
You do both . . .
Be the best!

Hannah Laing (14)
Badminton School

IF ONLY

If only there was not a mess,
In this world of ours.
No fighting, killing, hurting,
Just peace, no loneliness.

If only trees were made of sweets
And rivers ran with honey.
If only toys were everywhere
And we did not have money.

If only this could happen,
Although it never will,
But in my dreams these things occur,
These things my dreams do fill.

Miranda Robinson (12)
Badminton School

UNANSWERED QUESTIONS

Do the adults of today realise that we are their successors?
That when we succeed them a dismal world will remain,
Ruined by pollution from their nuclear factories?
Do they not realise,
Do they not care?

The countryside is being destroyed by plans for new housing,
Roadways and highways stretch to every town,
Providing a network but destroying the environment.
Do they not realise,
Do they not care?

We want a say in the currency of Britain,
We'll have to spend it when they're dead and gone,
So let us vote on it, hold a referendum,
Do they not realise,
Do they not care?

Police waste their time speed-trapping our elders,
Surely they'd be better off combating crime,
Leaving innocent people to live and be free.
Do they not realise,
Do they not care?

Natural disasters are waiting to happen
Earthquakes and hurricanes since the beginning of time,
People are dying while pointless wars are fought,
Do they not realise,
Do they not care?

The government of today is corrupt and hypocritical,
Breaking the laws that they installed,
If they vote on items, they should obey them,
Do they not realise,
Do they not care?

Eliza Bailey (12)
Badminton School

REFLECTED CRITICISM

You look so weak
You'll never be strong
In fact everything about you's . . . wrong!

Your nose is crooked
Your teeth ain't straight
But you can't put them right for it's far too late.

You're very pale
Almost white
Didn't you sleep well during the night?

You've got big bags
Under your eyes
But really to me that ain't no surprise.

I've seen you from something,
I've met you, I'm sure,
I'm positive, I'm certain I've seen you before.

I know you from somewhere
Oh who can you be?
Crumbs! By golly! That person's . . .
Me!

Eleanor Mills (13)
Badminton School

DAYDREAMING

Now I dream
Now I am with you
And at this point of the day I am happy.

Pure happiness without pain, worries or little nagging details
The idea of missing you is familiar and normal.
Memories of you haunt me
Now I am starting to believe them as real
And reality as fake.

The only thing now that makes me happy is the idea of you
And you are just a memory.

Slowly drifting and drowning in a sea of tears
Whispering and wailing the name of a lost love.

Now I am back to reality
But I can still hear that wail
Of a long lost love.

Miranda Porter (13)
Badminton School

OPEN EYES

An endless pit the future is,
Or so it seems to me;
Not dark or gloomy is our future,
Nor drenched in grime or pain.

To m ost when tomorrow comes,
It brings a fresh page to write on;
Smile! We all will have to take
The plunge into the future's pit.

But what does the future think
Of us invading its privacy?
Will we steal all its secrets
And throw them out to sea?

The future is still in front, so listen
To the future's voice and it will
Slowly wrap itself around you
and pull you gently in.

Anna Whicher (13)
Badminton School

SOMETHING'S WRONG

Something's wrong but I can't think what . . .
Is it your nose or your toes?
Is it your lips or your hips?
Is it your thighs or your size,
Or maybe it might be your eyes?
Could it possibly be your feet,
Or even the way you sleep?
Maybe it's your hair or your stare?
Maybe it's your ears or your fears?
Could it possibly be your tears?
I know it sounds crazy, but could it be your teeth?
Is it your heart or the way you think you're smart?
Is it your fingers or the way you like to linger?
Could it be that you're too keen,
Or that you have bad dreams?
I know,
I've got it,
It's the fact you're *not real.*

Katie Pendleton (12)
Badminton School

THE WATCH

Quizzical and new, the shiny face
Catches my eye
And holds it still in its wiry embrace

Your present is my future and past
Given hours ago,
In minutes you'll be back at last

Meanwhile I'm trapped in time -
Alarmed and frozen; seconds pass
Not waking me with bell or chime

No warmth or tact, no fear or hate
The heartless face just tells the truth
And indicates it's getting late

Unlike you the hands move on
But never leave me, then again
They never promise to return

Tick-tock tick-tock tick . . .
It stopped and you're not here!
Will there ever be time for us now?

Joanna Hunt (14)
Badminton School

ECHO

I wander into the dark cave,
water dripping from the mysteriously shaped icicles,
down into a puddle on the floor.

I look up and see green eyes,
glaring hard at me.
I am so frightened, I scream!

The eyes disappear and the sound of a little voice
is ringing in my ears,
but it's not mine.

It came from the never-ending hole in front of me,
coming towards me,
Like a voice from the future.

Antonia Kinlay (13)
Badminton School

AN IMAGE

When I wake up
and go to brush my teeth,
there's someone staring back at me.
I vaguely recognise them, from somewhere,
although I just can't quite remember where.
Was it a shop window in town
or the lake in the park?
She looks very pale
and quite frighteningly frail.
With long wisps of black hair curling and
twisted around her face,
blood red lips and dark eyes sparkling
like crystals.
She never talks to me,
she just stares intensely with an unhesitating gaze.
Almost curiously, as if she wants to find out more about me,
just by staring.
Maybe she'll be friends with me one day.

Erin Bishop (11)
Badminton School

A GIRL'S HEAD

Home, home, what a nice dream,
Wake up at school - nice thoughts all shattered.

Wish school food was something more exciting.
I don't have *that* teacher do I?
No! No! No!
Is every lesson going to be *this* long?

Wish I had my nail file -
Keep chipping my nails . . .

Has she not heard of tweezers?
Feel so sorry for her,
First day of school and all.

Got my bank card
And my PIN!
Put two and two together
And you get money!

Got to phone him -
No! He can phone me!

Why am I thinking about that?
What's it got to do with maths?

Georgia Smyth (13)
Badminton School

ME!

You look so ugly every day
You are so greedy every May.

You always have your glasses on
And your eyes are very small.

You look like a sleepy bear,
With two black bags and make me scared.

You look like a pot-bellied pig
Every time I see you, you have a round, round face.

Your face is too dirty,
I hope you washed your face before you saw me.

I have seen you every single day,
But I can't believe this is *me!*

Joanna Ha (12)
Badminton School

MY FUTURE

'What will my future be?' I asked
What will become of me?
Will I marry, have children
or live in single harmony?
Will I die young?
Or live past one hundred!
Oh, what will become of me?
Will I be a doctor, lawyer, artist, designer
or will I be unemployed?
No . . . not me!
Will my life be good all the way through,
or will it be full of misery?
Will I be queen, an empress or a millionairess,
or a humble cook for one of the three!
Will I slip away, peaceful and happy,
or die with terror in my eyes?
Will my spirit stay on Earth,
or soar up through the skies!
I ask again 'What will my future be?
And Grandma replies 'My dear, I really don't know!'

'Oh!'

Emily Baker (13)
Badminton School

FAIRIES

I still believe in the fairies
Who live beneath the old wall.
I see their footsteps in the dew
And hear their tiny calls.
When I wake up very early,
A little after dawn,
If I look from my window
I'll see the fairies on the lawn.
In-between the spiders' webs
All about the ground,
Darting through the flower beds
Flying all around.
Silvery, beautiful, delicate wings
And colourful flashes of light,
But if I even cough or stir
They're gone, into the night.

Alice Coombs (13)
Badminton School

WHAT WILL I BE?

Do people when they see me scream with fright or adoration?
Will the nation, when I'm older be thrilled to meet me,
Or will I be a down and out crawling in some street?
On my good days I see a cool girl, a popstar yet to be,
On others I see a shopkeeper, is working in WH Smiths for me?
Will I when I'm older let my scruffy side win,
Be dressed in rags looking for food in bins,
Or will I be a great barrister, who always wins?
Help me Lord, I really can't see, which is the real me?

Jesse Dyer (11)
Badminton School

MESSAGE TO THE BOYS

Shh! Dad's really ill,
I've left him in bed,
Please, creep about,
Please, don't shout.
Don't forget to brush your teeth,
Comb your hair,
Make your beds
And please, come quietly down the stairs.

Shh! Dad's really ill,
For once in your life, keep still,
Please, don't squabble,
Please, don't fight,
Just get yourselves organised in an orderly fashion,
Eat your breakfast,
Have a drink
And please, take the dirty plates over to the sink.

Shh! Dad's really ill,
Let's just leave him in bed,
Please, don't sing,
Please, don't tease,
Let's just get out of the house and leave him in peace,
Don't push,
Don't shove,
Please just collect your bags and leave the house.

Felicity Jell (13)
Badminton School

WHO OWNS THIS POEM?

Who owns time,
Who owns the sea,
Who owns the clouds,
Who owns me?

Is everything owned,
Or nothing at all?
Who owns a beetle?
We think we own it all.

Can you own the right to curse?
You can own the right to bless,
Can you own a feeling,
Anger, fear, happiness?

Does whoever owns you,
Own her and me,
Does whoever owns rain,
Own that which falls into the sea?

If ownership was banned,
Who would own the right to ban it?
If a building is to be built,
Can you own the right to plan it?

Do we own everything,
We think right,
I think not,
We have lost sight.

We want to own time,
We want to own the sea,
We want to own the clouds,
But, no one wants to own me.

Charlotte Wales (13)
Badminton School

WAR

Black trenches full of mud and rats,
The grime just hangs in the air giving off a deadly odour,
Misery lies around in the form of young men,
They carry green helmets and rucksacks filled to the brim
With ammunition,
They are so heavy it's a trial to walk.
A daring soldier scrambles over barbed wire sticking to a wall like ivy,
He trips, but carries on running through no-man's-land,
Then *bang* he stops short, falling to the ground with blood spurting
From his side.

The dreaded nuclear explosion awaits its time,
Aeroplanes screech overhead dropping bombs like flies,
Boom - the shock-wave radiates the earth,
Gas and smoke fill the sky, cloudy in the air.
Machine guns voice their last spurt through a shop window,
The smash of broken glass breaking the silence,
Falls on a mound of rubble giving a ghostly effect.

War is death like black is dark,
War's disloyalty makes human anger rise to the surface
And explode like bombs.
War lets the wicked scheme and have fun but the good suffer and die.
War leaves its mark like a stamp on a page,
Death and destruction are a sign that war has been staying once again.

Victoria Hunter Smart (13)
Badminton School

A Crayon

A crayon,
A mixture of different thoughts,
A different crayon, a different mood.

Instead of growing, a crayon shrinks,
The longer the crayon, the longer the life.

In a box there is jealousy, anger and greed,
With bright colours there is also happiness.

The crayon gets injured, it snaps,
Its life is over . . .

But when another crayon gets used,
There are new thoughts, moods and happiness.

Courtney Biles (14)
Badminton School

The Mirror

I tried to avoid it,
Well, just a little bit.
My mum said I would be sorry,
I was really starting to worry

And then, I took a step to the right,
I had a huge fright,
My mum was correct,
Now this action I do regret.

That one little action,
Just to the right a fraction,
Now I see,
The real me.

Lindsey Dunn (12)
Badminton School

TOMORROW

Tomorrow is a stranger
A mystery man, a thief,
An angel, an assassin
Tomorrow, well, who knows?

Tomorrow could be World War Three
Sneaking silently upon us
Like a thief in the night
Trespassing in unknown places.

Tomorrow fame could be mine
Or I could rule the world,
I could win the lottery
Or have the Queen for tea.

Tomorrow we might all perish
A nuclear bomb might explode
Cities crumble to dust
But a ray of hope there yet is.

Tomorrow will be beautiful
An evil forgotten and left
Life will be brilliant,
I hope, but I cannot know yet.

What will happen tomorrow?
No one on Earth can know
Will it be good or bad?
Tomorrow, well, who knows?

Kate Virgo (12)
Badminton School

MANKIND

Mankind came from Adam and Eve -
No, it did not!
Mankind came from Chinese tea leaves -
Maybe so, but . . .
Mankind came from monkeys -
I think not!
Mankind came from the oceans and seas -
No way!
Mankind came from aliens -
Yes or no?
Mankind came from the egg of a demon -
All of these could be true,
But the question I ask myself, is new.
It lurks in the depths of my mind . . .
What will become of mankind?

Chloë Hutchinson (13)
Badminton School

MY GUEST

Suddenly,
he flew through the gaps
of the door into my house,
like a guest.

An impolite, rude guest
without ringing the bell or knocking on the door,
I offered him a chair,
but he did not even look at me.

I tried to speak to him,
'Hi, how are you?' but
never an answer came,
only the 'whui, whui . . .' sound

And suddenly,
he is gone from the window
without saying goodbye!
An impolite, rude guest.

Josephine Lam (14)
Badminton School

FUTURE VOICES

The future may be bleak,
With litter and rubbish everywhere.
The voices of the future
Must make this change.

The future will hold many secrets,
Waiting to be unravelled.
The voices of the future
Must reveal the truth.

The future may be unhappy,
With sadness everywhere.
The voices of the future
Must provide joy.

The voices of the future must make the world a better place!

Victoria Hine-Haycock (13)
Badminton School

SILENCE

What is silence?
There can never be total silence,
You can always hear something,
Whether it be the scuttle of a mouse,
Or the wind in the trees.

If you can't get silence,
Then how do you know you love it,
Because people always say, 'What bliss'
This I never understand.

So my question stays unanswered,
What is silence?

Harriet Stone (14)
Badminton School

MY IMAGE

With blue eyes and blonde hair
With freckles each side of my nose,
With bulky eyebrows and thin eyelashes,
People never leer!

With small pierced ears,
With small tiny studs,
With my hair just about tied back
With bits hanging out!

Well my body's a different thing,
Small and thin, my feet small
And my hands small,
I am a small person in all!

Camille Parsons (11)
Badminton School

OLD MAN

Old man,
Leathery and tobacco
Smelling, his skin like
Parchment, a smooth
And yellowed map.
He reeks of history,
Days musty and waxed,
Days grainy and rich.
Pinked eyes, but
Eyes of wise, a
Self of wealth
And experience.
Tales from the depths
Of the seas, a mouth
Wrinkled, but which
Sings songs of antique
And irreplaceable beauty.
Standing in brightly
Lit shop, modern to strip
Him of his worth
His nervous hand
Fidgets his snow-white hair,
Trying to disguise
Baldness.
But no one's
Watching
And no one cares.

Sarah Thomas (16)
Badminton School

SPACE BUG

Hiya! My name's Mr Stute,
The first bug in a spacesuit.
I'm an astronaut's pet
But he's still got the cat to come yet.
I guess you could say I'm kinda strange,
But it's better than being *at home on the range!*
I'm 2cm long and 1cm tall,
I could've never ever climbed a wall.
But now that there's no gravity,
I'm not such a calamity.
My life has now been extended,
My special suit is patent pended.
I could be alive for another 20 years,
But someday it will all end in tears.
My wife and kids are coming soon,
They're taking the shuttle that goes via the moon.
Although my life sounds like fun,
There's lots of work that must be done.
I once got an electric shock,
Whilst fixing an automatic lock!
Bye, you know my name is Mr Stute,
I'm the worlds first bug in a spacesuit.

Emily Watson (13)
Badminton School

THE IMAGE

What is my reflection?
My image needed some detection
I don't like looking in the mirror!
It really makes me shiver
Just looking at my reflection
I need some perfection

A reflection is like a ghost
It haunts me the most
But sometimes I see
It is really me
Not just my reflection
Which needed some perfection.

Lydia Aston (11)
Badminton School

THINKING . . .

Thinking . . . an endless spiral of thoughts,
unable to stop yet to start is to be reborn.
Deep yet rich,
smooth yet harsh,
like a dream, secret and undisturbed,
a listed building,
full,
of change, never-ending
surprise.
A universe of sparkling stars, a galaxy of hope,
joy and sadness, sensitive but strong.
What is there like thinking?
Round and round a thought can go and yet
no conclusion ever drawn.
Real and unreal worlds cross over until two become
one.
There are no boundaries, rules or codes
but still not all is free
to be.
So are thoughts inside my head?

Helen Marshall (15)
Badminton School

HAZY DAYS

The sun bakes my slumber,
warming the skin
of careless limbs.
My eyes are slow
to let in the light,
dazzle striking blows
to the skull.
Hazy days breathe lethargy,
trickle like honey
along the spine.
Shimmering skies
and the whispers
of lazy insects
draw me towards life;
Yet still thick with traces
of a dream
Saying only what
I want to hear,
while bird-song falls
from the trees
like leaves.

Ellie Burt (17)
Badminton School

WHAT'S THE FUTURE?

Most people would say they can't tell the future,
Though some wouldn't think that at all.
Those people spend their time reading palms,
And looking into a crystal ball.

The future hasn't happened yet,
So I don't think someone should pay
To have their palms examined and read,
By a weird person who surely can't know what to say.

The future is quite far away,
No one knows what it might be
Or when it will suddenly come,
We will just have to wait and see.

So the future can be anything,
And when it arrives at last,
It quickly changes everything
Before it becomes the past.

Stephanie Gallia (13)
Badminton School

THE SOLDIER OF WAR

Bang! I hear the guns crack,
Bang! I feel footsteps behind my back,
Bang! I hear a million screams,
Bang! I see them in my dreams,
Bang! I see a tortured body fall,
Bang! I hear a crying child's call,
Bang! I see so many families lost,
Bang! They were killed at no cost,
Bang! I feel my blood pound,
Bang! I hear a siren's sound,
Bang! I feel the cold, grey lead,
Bang! I see my clothes run red,
Bang! I feel the stabbing pain,
Bang! I cry out in the pouring rain,
Bang! I fall to the muddy floor,
Bang! Soon my soul will be here no more,
Bang! Will this war never end,
Or is my country too hurt to mend?

Sophie Roberts (14)
Badminton School

LIFE

A complicated proverb
We are given it
But does anyone know how to use it?

There are no teachers or lessons to prepare us,
We must learn from experience
We never stop learning.

Think of life not as a gift
But as a question
And perhaps, perhaps death is the answer.

We spend our lives questioning, finding out,
We must harness the potential joy
And learn to use what we have been given.

I say one thing
And one thing only
Carpe diem!

Eleanor Hobhouse (13)
Badminton School

CRYSTAL BALL

Come and look in my crystal ball,
It will show you your feelings, thoughts and soul,
Your dreams and sorrows you will see,
Your childhood and what was meant to be.

It will call your ancestors from the past
And discuss how long your life should last.
Should you live another week or year?
By now, I see you tremble with fear.

Look at the crystal ball in my hand,
Showing your friends, your town and your land.
Your ambitions and hopes it will show
And the way your life will turn and go.

As the voices of your future face the sky
They grab your soul up and they fly.
For now you have heard their silent call
By viewing the mysterious crystal ball.

Masha Ooyevaar (13)
Badminton School

THE DANDELION

I start and end my life in the same kind of way.
As I lie low in the grass among the daisies and buttercups
                                    I hear the children play.
Happy noises, noises of playing wild and free!
Then the ground trembles and my weak green stem starts to shake.
That's it! That's it! I know what's coming!
I shall be no more!
One o'clock, two o'clock, three o'clock, four o'clock!
Scattered into many pieces flying, soaring high and free.
Across towns, cities, meadows and fields.
I hear the song of birds and pass the squirrels eating sweet chestnuts.
Then the roaring, bustling wind stops!
I glide, like a snowflake from the sky, gently bouncing to the ground.
I land in a hedgerow and there I start to grow again.
One o'clock, two o'clock, three o'clock, four o'clock!
Whoosh, up I go again!

Laura Mackenzie (13)
Badminton School

SPLASH

Splash!
Wow! It's cold! Wait -
Is my mask and my reg in place?
Hold on! Please wait!
No, stop! Breath deeply and slowly.
No! Don't go yet - I haven't . . .
I haven't cleaned my ears.

Now we are going down.
I watch my depth gauge:
1, 2, 3, 4, 5, 6, 7, 8, 9, 10, 11, 12, 13, 14, 15
It has stopped,
I have hit the bottom
It is so good . . .
It is so cold
Ok! Time to clear my mask and ears.

Now I have done that, it's time to play!
So many colours,
So many things to see . . .
Look over there! A star fish!
A crab!
Oops! I forgot -
Check your air; Help!
It is below 50 bars
Fin up and up.

Camilla Ayrton (13)
Badminton School

OUTSIDE THE WINDOW

I like sitting next to the window,
Especially at night, when I am alone.
There is always so much to hear and to see,
Whistle of the wind and whispering of the trees.

The view I look at is always beautiful,
A mixture of happiness, calmness and sorrow.
If you look carefully at this amazing scene,
It's like a painting with shadows of leaves.

As the raindrops fall from the sky,
Tears start rolling down my eyes.
Missing someone I must be,
Parents perhaps, or friends it could be.

Memories flash clearly in my head
Every night when I lie on my bed.
My family, my friends and everyone I know
Out of my head will never go.

Whenever I'm sad, whenever I'm down,
Up I get and turn around.
The Northern Star which shines so bright
Looks and smiles at me every night.

This calms me down and cheers me up,
Then I'll give my eyes a gentle rub,
Try to think in a nice bright way,
Tomorrow will be a brand new day.

Celeste Luk (14)
Badminton School

WHY CAN'T I DECIDE?

You're so small,
Oh sorry that's her,
You are quite tall,
I suppose.

Your eyes are all green,
Oh sorry that's him,
Your eyes are blue,
I suppose.

Your skin's so crinkly,
Oh sorry that's you,
Your skin's okay,
I suppose.

Your hair's so greasy,
Oh sorry that's me,
Your hair's fine really,
I suppose.

Oh I wish you'd decide,
Can't you make up your mind,
Actually don't bother,
I don't want to know!

Elizabeth Rich (11)
Badminton School

SELF IMAGE

You look quite small
But your eyes are so bright
You look so shy
But you are quite nice
You're friendly and jolly
With a great big smile

But in the mornings when you get up
Your hair is a mess
You are grumpy and tired
You should have stayed in bed
For another half hour.

Kathryn Stoddart (11)
Badminton School

THE FAIRY ON THE CHRISTMAS TREE

I am the fairy on top of the Christmas tree,
Everybody likes me except for me,
I was in a factory not long ago,
Now I'm in a puddle, wet as my friend Mo.

My first home was fun,
I got cuddled by Mum,
Until one day,
I got thrown away.

I got found by a man
And here I am,
On top of a tree,
Which is scary you see.

I'm covered in lights
And I don't like heights,
Tomorrow is the day when the children will come
And open their presents from Dad and Mum.

So here you see,
I'm as unfortunate as can be,
When Christmas Eve comes again,
The kids will make me go insane.

Joanna Caroline Ritchie (11)
Badminton School

GROWING UP

I used to be quiet and shy
and anything would make me cry,
I am much braver now I'm older
and I look and feel much bolder.

I used to be very plain
and now I don't look much the same,
I am much taller and bigger,
but I don't know what to say about my figure.

I used to have a very small nose
and tiny little piggy toes,
but now I'm older my mouth's too wide
and I just don't know where to hide!

Lizzy O'Neill
Badminton School

CHRISTIANITY

Immortality, oh sweet immortality,
Caressing me with her mystic morality.
I'm completely relaxed without a care,
In a world beyond happiness, free from despair.

Sensibility, oh sweet sensibility,
Clutching my worries with her loving security.
I'm utterly defensible, upheld by faith,
In a world revealing trust, that is suddenly magically safe.

Serenity, oh sweet serenity,
Crystallising me from every whiff of gluttony.
I'm fully evolved into something good,
In a world where I'm living, just as I should!

Sophie Cran (13)
Badminton School

ME

I wonder if there is a perfect me,
with straight and bright white teeth.

If there is a perfect me,
I should have sparkling eyes
and beautiful eyelashes.

Dry lips and flat nose,
untidy teeth and tiny eyes
that is what I've got!

But in some ways I am good,
I'm small, I have nice hair and long fingers.

The thing I am glad about me
is that I'm not the perfect me.

Joyce Lau (12)
Badminton School

THE VOICE OF THE FUTURE

The voice of an angel is a voice of grace,
The voice of a wizard is a voice of charm,
The voice of a witch is a voice of enchantment,
The voice of a king is a voice of wisdom,
The voice of a ghost is a voice of the dead,
The voice of a god is a voice of holiness,
The voice of a fairy is a voice of fantasy,
The voice of the future is a voice unknown to man.

Catherine Richardson (14)
Badminton School

8.00AM ON AN ICY MORN

The whole beauty of the experience is unknown to some,
Waiting and wondering if there is ever going to be a sun.
The smell and the taste and the feel of the ice,
It's just plain torture, take my advice.

The rules of conduct in this solitary place,
Lets the cold air move into your space.
You mustn't move or walk around,
It's best not to make a sound.

So you sit and you stare at the frosted grass,
You know that yours will surely be last.
But still I know it just might come,
Maybe 15 minutes an hour for some.

The ice pricks your skin like 1000 pins,
Maybe a punishment for all your sins.
The way that you yearn for some heat is just torture,
Your fingers go numb and your eyes start to water.

Where I am, who I am with,
You're beginning to suss,
It's simple now really, where is that bus?

Annabelle Walter (12)
Badminton School

ME!

I looked in the mirror this morning
To see that the day was dawning
My eyes were black, my hair was a mess,
But so, I couldn't care less.
Give it a brush, have a blink,
That might change the way people think.

When the horses decide that,
They need some attention I will change into my tat,
Put my hair up in a mess
But I couldn't care less
I can always try tomorrow!

Victoria Stanley (11)
Badminton School

THE ANGEL OF THE FUTURE AND HEAVEN

Staring from a distance,
I gazed in bewilderness at her radiant aura.
She stood tall and proud with no faults to condemn her.
Her hair was like a golden stream
That lapped against her shoulders in the wind,
Each golden piece of hair added to her complexion.
As the sun's beams of richness glisten onto her composition,
Her eyes twinkle and reflect her view of the future,
Which was so beautiful as it reflected her well-being.
The pigment of her skin was so beautifully tanned,
It was as soft as soapstone yet as hard as steel
To protect her from maleficence.
Her cherry colour lips spoke the words of a gracious
And giving soul:
'The future is a land of dreams, it is a doorway to
Heaven, never neglect it or try to prevent it. It will
Materialise and when it does tolerate and enjoy it.'

She slowly drifted away,
To her heaven I presume
And from where she stood grew a cherry tree,
It blossomed and matured, beautifully.
When I looked at the tree
I saw my heaven and future shielding me.

Melanie Carrington (13)
Badminton School

I AM NOTHING

I am nothing,
nothing at all,
nothing but the tiniest
speck on a wall.

I wish I could dance
and act in a theatre,
I wish I could run
and be a pop singer.

I am nothing,
nothing at all,
nothing but a
speck on a wall.

People tease me,
because I wear glasses,
they call me metal teeth,
because of my braces.

I am nothing,
nothing at all,
nothing but a speck,
a speck on a wall.

Olivia Prichard (11)
Badminton School

BLIND

I shut my eyes,
Will they open again?
I edge them slowly towards the light,
Is this the ending of the night?

I live in darkness,
Exist by touch,
The smells and sounds may not be much,
But this is the world in which I exist,
The wind and the breeze make me feel I've been kissed.

Eleanor McNaughtan (13)
Badminton School

DISNEYLAND

Candyfloss fumes and smoke,
It sticks in your throat.
The taste of the air,
Enticing you, enclosing you,
Making you feel sick.
Fireworks go bang! Screams echo,
Constant racket as people talk.
Annoying theme park music,
The buzz of flies.
Smells you like, smells you hate,
Mixed up in a sickening concoction.
Food, smoke and sick,
People milling, waiting for rides,
Some twist, some turn,
It's your choice.
Parades - someone tall in front,
Blocking your view of the fun.
Don't step here . . . or there,
It's not pleasant.
Petrol and food covers the ground,
Squish, squash,
Every step you take.

Lucy Simms (12)
Badminton School

CHRISTMAS AT MY HOUSE

Taste
The cold wintry morning,
Which lingers in the air,
Also the pine from the tree,
Which is a taste I can't describe.

Hear
The animals barking and miaowing,
As they come and greet us,
The opening of the presents,
As they crinkle into a ball.

Smell
The newly opened books,
The porridge for our breakfast
And the sweet smell of cats,
Who have been snuggled on my bed.

See
The decorations glittering on the tree,
The table laid for dinner,
Under the tree there are more presents,
I wonder who they could be for?

Touch
Feel the bitter air,
As I walk through the snow,
The coldness comes through your gloves,
As I attempt to build a snowman.

Sophie Weerawardena (12)
Badminton School

THE SHOW

Stars of light shimmer,
I have to focus.
Although there's something wrong, I'm sure,
But what?
I look at the audience, they're glaring as if I look odd,
The music starts, the lights go on,
Hang on I've heard this music before,
That note,
What does it mean?
Of course, it's my cue to sing,
I open my mouth,
But no sound comes out.
I try a bit harder
And then at last, a note.
I carry on,
The crowd is cheering,
Waving their arms and screaming.
It's all like a dream,
What was I fearing?
Suddenly the music stops,
I run off stage.
I hear a big roar behind me from the crowd,
I run to my dressing room and look in the mirror.

I don't look odd, just a little flushed,
Nothing much.
A voice interrupts me,
'Kathy you were amazing out there,
You've got the job!'
The door shuts and I stare into the mirror,
Startled.

Natasha Lawless (11)
Badminton School

THINKING OF YOU

When I think of you,
I think of the zoo,
Because you're mad, weird
And strange too.

When I'm trying to get to bed,
Your jokes stick in my head,
They're really really not funny,
They're always just about money.

You always get your own way
And you're always mean to that girl Faye,
You're always picking your nose, *yuk!*
And that thumb you suck.

Altogether you're just weird
And I think I'll stay away.
Don't take offence,
I really don't mean it in a mean way.

Camilla Voke-Jewitt (11)
Badminton School

IMAGES OF WHAT?

An old man, with a long, white beard,
Sitting up there, on a cloud,
Or a big, orange blanket,
Keeping you warm, safe and content.

A deity with chinking, dangling necklaces,
Some have ones of gold, others ones of beads.
Someone riding in a chariot,
Pulling the sun.

A person, sitting lotus,
Eyes wide, clear and kind
A holy presence, somewhere,
You have to know it to find it.

So many images, none of them right,
Yet none of them wrong,
Which one shall I choose?

Nadia Kevlin (11)
Badminton School

ON A BOAT

The cold damp air,
Tasting the wet salt in your mouth.
The icy waters sloshing up onto you,
The swells of the sea bring you up and down,
The lashing sea disappearing into the grey fog.
Seeing nothing and not knowing what's happening next,
The massive booms of the thunder.
Hearing the shouts of the crew as they spot a big wave,
The distinct salt smell wafting up from the deep sea,
Smelling the petrol as the boat chugs along.

Abbie Vallance (12)
Badminton School

MY SENSES

See
Making a cake is the sort of thing that makes a mess,
Also when the mixture gets less and less.
When you see the soft brown sauce,
You feel as if you could eat a horse.

Touch
As I run down the path,
The squelch of mud beneath my feet,
Sinking deeper, deeper,
Splodge, right in front of my face all the mud goes.
Brown as a cake I go back,
I'm fearing it as I'll get a smack.

Taste
Only a spoonful Mum said,
Then it's time to go to bed.
The chocolate running down my throat,
Warms me up inside my coat.

Hear
Hear the milkman coming down the path,
I had to rush out of the bath.
A sudden thump on the floor
And at last I get to the door.
He gives me a wink and a sigh
And with a slight cough he says 'Goodbye.'

Smell
In the meadow there's a lovely smell,
It also smells a bit like a fell.
In the meadow I lie,
Watching the clouds go by.

Sophie Cheeseman (12)
Badminton School

HAMMY THE HAMSTER

A bristle of whiskers,
A flurry of fur,
A goldish colour,
Yes, that's her!

Four tiny paws,
Two little eyes,
Black as jet,
I wonder why!

Her little tail,
It is so sweet.
If she's good,
I'll give her a treat.

Her golden fur,
Is as soft as silk.
Her two long teeth,
They're as white as milk.

Her little pink nose
Sniffs on the go,
With her little whiskers,
They're like thorns outside a rose.

I love my little hamster,
With her teeth like snow,
Her little pink nose
And those whiskers on the go!

Amanda McDowall (11)
Badminton School

I'M A LONELY RIVER

Look at me, I'm so lonely,
Nobody flows with me.
Maybe it's my looks, my blue!
Look at my green.
I'm so lonely.

Look at me, I'm so lonely,
Nobody likes me.
Only my mummy loves me.
She's happy at the mouth, but me . . .
I'm so lonely.

Look at me, I'm so lonely,
Nobody flows with me.
Ducks and birds ride on me, it's horrible!
But it's my only company,
I'm so lonely.

Look at me, I'm so lonely,
Nobody likes me.
It's because of my shape.
I'm sometimes straight but other times I wiggle about.
I'm so lonely.

Look at me, I'm so lonely,
When will I dry out? How long will I exist?
I'm so lonely.

Look at me, I'm so lonely
Nobody flows with me,
But now I'm all alone in the sea.
Mummy, Daddy, where are you?
I'm so lonely.

Ellen Li (11)
Badminton School

CLEANING OUT THE POND

The water splashes everywhere,
It goes into your mouth and your hair,
You spit it out,
But the taste lingers,
It tastes like sick.

A splash as the net hits the water,
Ripples appear as fish swim
Like prisoners to the border,
The frog croaks to its mate,
The buzz of the insects.

The water stinks like a rubbish heap,
The seaweed reminds you of the sea,
The smells get up your nose,
The unmistakable smell of mint,
As you brush against the rockery.

The pond is like an underground station
Everyone rushing about like matron,
The frogs jump when the net comes near,
The fish swim to the surface
And then disappear.

As my hand goes into the freezing cold,
The slimy seaweed folds
And raps around my arm,
I grab something
And bring it up,
It's slimy and soft,

A dead frog!

Amy Binley (12)
Badminton School

SENSUAL BONFIRE

Golden sparks,
Rising flames,
Glowing embers
Against a blanketed sky.

I taste the air overflowed with ash,
The decaying leaves which odour the air,
The smoke, flowing past in the wind.

I smell the soot infested trees,
The candy all around me,
The old, dead leaves, resting by my feet.

I hear the crackling of the bonfire,
The music coming from the fairground,
The sound of laughter, travelling past my ears.

I see the glowing fire, smoke rising from it,
The people running around in excitement,
The ancient vibes of the towering trees.

I feel the warmth of my gloves,
The smoke in my eyes,
The cool breeze on my cheeks

Why? Because it's the sensual fire.

Charlotte Turner (12)
Badminton School

MY WHITE CHRISTMAS

You can taste the air,
Thin, icy, cool and clear.
The fresh winter breeze,
Freezes your mouth and burns your throat.

You can hear the laughter and joy in children's voices
As they open their doors to a white Christmas,
The robins are chirping merrily,
They too are delighted.

You can smell the aroma of roast turkey,
Roasting away in every house on every street,
The scent of pine needles scattered far and wide.

You can see snowmen,
A personality all of their own,
Full of character,
A layer of snow on your clothes, still warm.

You touch the snow,
It slips through your hand as shy as ever,
Numbing your fingers,
Today is my white Christmas.

Kate Shilton (12)
Badminton School

THE STREETS IN HONG KONG

Taste
The smoke from the engines of the car
Which fill the air
The taste of the dry
Burning atmosphere.

Hear
Horns beep in the streets
People talking
Music from the stores
Which drift out.

Smell
The lovely baked cakes
From the stores
The sewage and the rubbish
All clattered among the walls.

Touch
Feel the hot air around you
Following you everywhere
The burning hand rails
In the streets of Hong Kong.

Suzanna Pang (12)
Badminton School

TURKEY

I taste   The humid air,
The sweat that trickles down my forehead;
The chlorine of the pool
Mixed with salt from the Mediterranean.

I hear   The distant rumble of the sea,
The dog barking at our arrival,
The stuttered English of Mustafa our maid
And the jolt of the van engine.

I smell   The pure heat that lingers around us,
The dust that the van throws up,
The tropical plants nearby.

I see   The beautiful villa,
The rustic couple standing before us,
The picturesque swimming pool
And far in the distance, the sparkling ocean.

I feel   The scorching ground that burns your feet
Through your shoes,
The cool door knob
And all around me,
The relaxing air of my holiday dream.

Arabella Rowe (12)
Badminton School

THE GYPSY WOMAN

Jingle jangle, jingle jangle,
The sounds of her rattling bangles,
As she lights her scented incense sticks,
And then her many candles.

Her wispy hair has grown silver with age,
But here and there a black strand remains,
Infused with threads of soft candlelight,
As she looks outside into the cool autumn night.

A swish of her long and tasselled black skirt,
Sweeps the floor of its dust and dirt,
As she glides with mystique through the old caravan,
Weeping and mourning the death of her man.

Her shawl grew deep through the tears she wept,
Her long silver earrings felt cold on her neck,
And just as she turned to wipe her eyes,
A vision appeared and answered her cries.

A man - her husband, stood and smiled,
He said he'd always be with her, watching and waiting,
And all the while she must carry on, never wither.

With that, she brightened and burnt some oils,
Heather, lavender and rose,
She peered into her crystal ball,
And put aside her sorrows.

Jingle jangle, jingle jangle,
The sounds of her clinking bangles,
As she lights her scented incense sticks,
And then her many candles.

Caroline King (13)
Badminton School

I LIE AWAKE

I lie awake,
It's so dark,
There's no one awake except me.
I hear a creaking floorboard.
It's coming from upstairs.
It can't be coming from upstairs.
All there is up there is a big, black room with boxes.
Why would anyone go upstairs?
It's so dark and scary.
Nobody ever dares to go upstairs.
There isn't anyone upstairs!
I'm imagining it all.
Anyway, only my dad would be brave enough to go up there.
There's a man behind my door.
I can see him standing there.
I don't think he knows I know he is there.
I can't see his eyes.
I slowly shrink away under the duvet.
I don't want him to know I'm here.
My heart is pounding so loudly
I wonder if he can hear it.
I secretly reach for the light -
Snap!
The light goes on and my head pops out.
A sigh of relief.
It was only my dressing gown!

Elizabeth Peers (13)
Badminton School

WAR IS...

The trenches are covered in muddy water.
It rained last night.
It stinks of dirty rats and dead bodies.
There is not many of us left now
And the ones that are, are fighting till their death.
We fight through the night and through the day,
Until all is left is bones and blood.

Nuclear bombs are around us,
Nuclear bombs are everywhere.
Death at the press of a button.
Aeroplanes sawing through the air like an eagle.
Battle ships racing through the choppy water.
Waiting to hit their target.
Everyone wants to be more powerful than each other.

All wars cause tragedies, death and pain.
So many young souls are lost,
Fighting for their own country.
The bodies of unknown men,
Lie there lifeless.
The scenes they had seen there could never be,
Washed away from their minds.

Clementine Balfour (13)
Badminton School

THE PRODUCTION

The dust,
Floating around me
As I recite my words
And move around.

The rustling
Of the programmes,
As the pages get flicked,
Whilst scanned through by beady eyes.

The polish
From the old wooden floor,
As I shuffle
From side to side.

The audience
Gazing back,
As I sing and act,
Under the spotlight.

The velvet curtains,
Touching and feeling them,
As I bow down.

I hear the applause,
And grin.

Rosamund Williams (12)
Badminton School

CORNWALL

Splash, splash, splash,
go the waves
creaking on the mouldy breakwater.

The sea, the sea, the sea,
turquoise and white
roaring like an angry lion.

Bob, bob, bob,
go the boats
swaying like washing on a line.

Salt, salt, salt,
is what I can taste
strong and dehydrating.

Caw, caw, caw,
I hear the seagull
swooping and diving above me.

Sand, sand, sand,
lying on the golden beach
scratching and squeaking under my feet.

Cornwall, Cornwall, Cornwall,
it brings back memories
The seas, the sand, the sights
Cornwall, Cornwall, Cornwall.

Victoria Baker (13)
Badminton School

WHAT DO I LOOK LIKE?

What do I look like?
I wish I knew
It's so unfair
These lids of blue.

They hide the world
From me, you know
But something tells me
I've still got to go.

I wonder if people
Look at me
And stare because
I cannot see.

I wish I had
A favourite colour
But all I ever see
Is the same blue cover.

I speak to other people
Who say they are blind
And all they see
Is red all the time.

I wish I had
Two normal eyes
And lived like people
Who have normal lives.

Miranda Mason (11)
Badminton School

DREAMS

Drifting off to sleep,
Where might my mind wander?
Maybe happy things,
Or even cruel things,
Where do dreams come from?
Is it like living in an imaginary land,
Or is it just trying to solve that maths equation?
Is it a part of our mind that we just haven't discovered?
Do we drift off into the clouds,
Or do we meet elves and fairies?
Do we really dream?

Debbie Yates (13)
Badminton School

MY FUTURE CAREER

Park
Park keeper
Lovely big house
Everything within my reach
Wheelchair ramps, lots of paths
Huge trees, lovely flowers
Feed the ducks
Children play
Tidy.

Jamie Baseley (12)
Burton Hill House School

FOOTBALL POEM!

I like Leeds United
They are great!
I feel excited when they score;
The crowd go absolutely wild.
When Man U score it suddenly goes amazingly quiet.
Half-time, it was 1-1.

The second half -
The teams run out of the tunnel
The fans roar!
They kick-off with a bad start
Two players are sent off
The crowds boo the referee
Leeds are on a good run . . .
They score!
The crowd shout and cheer.
Five minutes left
Lee Bowyer shoots from 30 yards
He scores for Leeds!
The whistle blows and the Leeds crowd go wild!
3-1.

Martin Nicholls (13)
Burton Hill House School

I GO FOR A WALK

I look outside it's snowing,
Quickly and with great excitement
I run down the stairs two at a time.
I find my boots and pull them on,
Tying the laces up tightly.
I run upstairs
To look for my coat
I can't find it
I grab my mum's and button it up.
Once downstairs again
I call for the dog
'Here Scruffy, come on boy, walkies.'
He comes running to me
I put on his lead,
I open the door and
I go for a walk.

Philippa Jeacocke (12)
Churchill Community School

THE LIFESAVER

As I jump elegantly over the waves,
Flipping my flippers they hit with a *splash!*
My curved body glides through the air
And my dorsal fins curve to one side.
My bottled nose softly touches the calm sea.
I'm a gentle giant with my pointed fins
And my acrobatic displays and my joyful leaps
Make me a proud but curious mammal.
I quickly cascade back into the clear water
And gently glide to join my school,
Alert and aware that someone's in trouble.

Stephanie Hawkesby (12)
Churchill Community School

THE CROCODILE

In forest glade a delicate deer
Sips from a leafy pool.
Its ears and eyes twitch alert,
Unaware of the predators that live there.
The sneaky crocodile is aware of his lunch,
Cunningly drawing closer.
Nearly there,
The deer runs,
But it is too slow.
As he grabs the deer,
With his teeth and claws,
Dragging it into the water,
It's too late now,
The deer is dead,
From the death roll.

Sophie Cooling (12)
Churchill Community School

DOLPHINS

I'm a subdued grey-coloured dolphin
With a dark dorsal cape,
I've got a rounded head and body,
And a distinct beak with a melon crease.
I swim with my friends in groups
Sometimes we swim in front of boats
Or sometimes we jump with the waves
Hitting the water in our acrobatic way.

Lori Gilbert (13)
Churchill Community School

THE PANTHER

The sleek slim slender shadow of the panther
Stalks through the night
The moonlight glints brightly on its coat,
Then the shadow cat spots its prey
Its whiskers tense as if they could cut through steel,
Its ears prick towards the stars,
Its padded leather soles make no noise on the floor
Its lungs fill with wet warm air,
The shadow leaps onto a branch
But no noise can be heard,
Its prey starts to move on
Darting, weaving through the undergrowth,
Growl! Yelp! Sleeping birds fly!
There's a bright light in the shadow cat's eyes!

Matthew Earley (12)
Churchill Community School

RUGBY

Arms lift
Throw ball
Run on
Catch ball
Trip over
Drop ball
Get up
Run on
Tackle Becky
Take ball
Run on
Touch down
Score!

Emma Briggs (12)
Churchill Community School

THE SCARED HEDGEHOG

Buried under a pile of rotten leaves, safely embedded
in a small black hole,
The hedgehog shuffles,
The leaves move and a mountain falls down,
The hedgehog is uncovered,
His black, wet nose snuffles to make sure everything is safe,
Then he cautiously goes from the cushioned, flat leaves to leave them to
blow with the gentle spring wind,
His behaviour slow and strong.
He shuffles towards the grass in the garden, his home,
On the grass he looks for food and finds and eats some wriggly worms
covered in mud,
Then suddenly he spots his enemy, a fox!
The fox's bright eyes glare and spot the hedgehog,
Then the hedgehog curls and rolls up in a tight ball just as the fox
shoots to kill.
The fox knocks the hedgehog with his cold nose, moving it like a
snooker ball.
The hedgehog stays tight and wrapped and slowly the fox moves away
leaving a brown lump,
The hedgehog looks and spots the fox once again and looks around for
safety,
Then he spots a hedge of brambles and heads surprisingly fast leaving a
small mouse hole.
With a shake of scaredness and a full stomach
He drags leaves together in a ring with his claw and curls up in a warm
ball, tucking his head underneath and falling slowly, slowly to sleep,
Going to sleep once again, another time as the seasons go by,
The season is over and will return once again.

Anna Blackshaw (12)
Churchill Community School

SOCCER

Great shot
Moves fast
The fast ball
Through the air
Hands raise
But why?
The ball
Curls away
From the
Stranded keeper.
Lowers head
Counts the score
Whistle blows
Missed the chance
To win the match
And the league.

Henry Page (13)
Churchill Community School

ACTION REPLAY

I wake up
My eyes open
I wake up

I open my eyes
I turn over
I stretch my legs
I wake up

I open my eyes
I rub the sleep away
I turn over
I dream
I stretch my legs
They feel like logs
I yawn
I wake up.

Joe Larder (12)
Churchill Community School

LOST IN THE GARDEN

I'm lost in the garden,
I don't know what to do,
It's like a forest, the grass is so long,
I am still only young and small,
The bushes are so big like they've never been cut,
But then the door opens,
Like a burst of light in the dark.
I get a burst of hope, a person with such long legs,
But then, ding, dong, the doorbell goes.
All hope is gone forever now,
But, suddenly, I'm picked up from behind,
Who is it?
Is it someone to take me away?
Oh, it's just Mum, I'm saved at last!
The ordeal over, in my house I shall stay;
Just in time for bed!

Luke Hewitt (11)
Churchill Community School

THE DEER

In the wood on the hill,
something is awakening,
getting up and leaping away.
A deer.

The dark coldness
gets to me as I walk along.
Then it's there on the top of the hill,
The king of the wood.

I creep towards it,
its eyes are sparkling,
it looks for the lost sound,
and moves a bit closer.

Its ears are twitching,
what did it hear?
It chews some berries,
slowly round and round.

It breaks a twig,
which snaps loudly.
Its nose reaches the air,
and it slowly leaps away.

Pollyanna Bryant (12)
Churchill Community School

THE WHALE

This huge mammal gliding gracefully through the water
Its perfect rounded fins pushing away the water.
The squeaking of its loud voice echoes through the ocean.
Then suddenly it turns and sharply jumps through
the water into the air.
It slices back
Splash!
Its tail drums on the ocean bed and pushes away all small fishes.
The deep blue water shines as the sunrays come through.
The whale gives a last squeak happily.
It gently swims off to find its family.

Sima Madanipour (12)
Churchill Community School

WINTER

Winter has come
Ground covered with white.
Snowflakes are falling,
River frozen hard.
Thud on the ground,
Snowballs fly high.
Snowman dressed up,
Sledging all around.
Twenty-fifth is coming.
Streets sparkle with light.
Friends and family visiting,
Giving presents and gifts.
Snowflakes have melted,
Flowers come again
Spring has arrived.

Tina Lau (11)
Churchill Community School

THE JAGUAR

I open the garage door and take
a glimpse of the mean machine.

I sit on the soft leathery seat,
I turn the key.

The sweet engine purrs like a cat
and revs louder and louder.

The car skids on my drive's gravel.
I accelerate and speed round the corner,
the engine revving higher and higher.

The dark road is lit with lamp posts.
I speed faster and faster, I see
a strange black object on the road.

Then the lights of my car illuminate
a face . . . I screech on the brakes!

Jack Fraser (11)
Churchill Community School

DREAM WORLD

In my dream world,
Flowers would bloom all year round,
There would be birds as tame as pets,
And a perfectly crystal-clear stream.

In my dream world,
Plums would be ripe on the tree,
Little white lambs would jump high,
In a landscape of rolling green hills.

In my dream world,
Trees would be reds, golds and greens,
Rabbits would roam all the hills,
And white fluffy clouds would rule blue skies.

In my dream world,
Grass would be greener than green,
Fish would splash deep in the ponds,
And snow-topped mountains would tower high.

Lorna Wilson (12)
Churchill Community School

MY DREAM

One of my dreams was when
I was a cat and my friend
was a cat too. It was luxury
being a cat because we slept,
then we messed around and
eventually went outside.

As soon as we got outside,
I felt like I was squashed
like an ant because
everything was so big.
I leapt onto the wall but
suddenly fell down.
I woke up and never knew
what happened next . . .

Samantha Parsons (12)
Churchill Community School

FROM COCOON TO BUTTERFLY

Tiny delicate butterfly,
Relying on the wind to carry it along,
Taking its first flight from the cocoon,
Fluttering gently.
Such delicate wings, so easily broken,
Gravity pulling it down to a small drop and then up again,
Fighting hard against the whipping wind,
Fluttering, flittering, in the deep, blue sky,
Falling onto a lime-green leaf,
Spreading out its colourful wings, to pose in the hot summer's sun,
Then off again into the open air that is mild and warm,
The butterfly has entered the world,
Flying over the uneven, muddy surface of the ground,
Everlasting, forever-living butterfly.

Joanna Clarke (12)
Churchill Community School

SCORING

Throw ball forward,
Strength from arms
Force legs into a run
Grind to a halt
Out of breath
Turn last ounce of energy
Into an interception
Hands grasp ball
Arms stretch
Into a throw
Cheers in ears
Ball goes through, rewarded,
A goal!

Sarah Portas (12)
Churchill Community School

FOX SONNET

The vixen runs through the woods in a rush,
Trying to save her beautiful big brush,
Runs to her young and puts them in her lair,
It is the foxhunters they cannot bear,
If they were to be caught they would be dead,
The really vicious dogs run straight ahead,
They are safe until the humans come by,
They move to a bush for the fox is sly,
The hunters haven't a clue where they are,
The men turn back to their villages far,
The foxes are safe for another day,
They come out of their hiding place and play,
They snap at butterflies and leap and jump,
They wear themselves out and fall in a clump.

Daniel Harris (12)
Churchill Community School

CHILDREN'S PARTIES

Ring! Ring! Goes the front doorbell,
Oh look, it's Chantelle.
People all come, come, come, come,
They all like to have fun.

Cakes and ice-cream,
When dinner time comes
Children scream,
Wanting iced buns.

Lots of presents I always get,
Oh yes, but don't forget
The one in the cupboard last of all
The surprise we've all been waiting for.

Bella-Louise Durbin (11)
Churchill Community School

LOST IN THE DARKNESS

I stand there in the dark,
All alone, no one to talk to,
I hear grasshoppers everywhere,
I'm scared, I'm scared.

I see the light of the lighthouse
Flooding out to sea
To warn the boats of icebergs
That may be lurking nearby.

I hear the sound of people
Having lots of fun,
I wish I wasn't here, all alone,
I'm scared, I'm scared.

Amy Orgee (11)
Churchill Community School

PANDA

Panda up the tree
Looking for some fun
As well as keeping watch
For anacondas and all other predators
The big, fluffy bear trying to catch some leaves
Hanging for dear life
Waiting for some friends
Poor little endangered bears.

Jason Campbell (11)
Churchill Community School

THE AFTERLIFE

I wonder what I'll be,
In the afterlife?
Will I be a buzzy bee
Or, hold the subtle knife?

Will I be a meal?
Will I be a sweet?
I'd never be a cat,
Too much pressure on my feet.

Perhaps I'll be a cheetah,
Or will I be a dog?
I'd never be a sailor
Too much writing in my log.

Perhaps I'll be a pen
Perhaps I'll be a pool
I'd never be a haunted house
Unless it had a ghoul.

Will I be a fireman?
Will I have a job?
I'd never be a tennis star
I just couldn't do a lob.

I wonder what I'll be?
Will I live in Fife?
I really, really hope
I like the *afterlife!*

Kate Lynham (12)
Churchill Community School

THE CROCODILE

The deadly croc lies wallowing in the water.
Its large, long body invisible to the eye.
Only its lazy eye above the river
A dark mean colour watching its prey.

It quietly creeps making just a ripple,
The food not knowing its life at risk.
The croc meets the land, its head in view
Then the foot, the leg, the victim still unaware.

As it carefully moves inch by inch,
Making no more of a stir, than a mouse.
It creeps . . . and pounces,
The now lifeless victim, but a meal to a croc.

The deadly crocodile still chewing,
Another life devoured, another day over.
Tomorrow, a deer or a lame hyena,
Innocent and harmless, but something to eat . . .

Tom Coombes (13)
Churchill Community School

AFRICA

Africa, where the sea is blue and the air is warm,
Where the roads are dusty and the people friendly,
Where lions prowl and antelopes leap,
But also where the hunters sleep.

Where the hunters sleep and wake at dawn,
To prey on the creatures,
To stalk and murder innocent animals,
And act more or less like cannibals.

Zebras run and elephants charge,
When the hunter comes into their path,
The bullets fire, the rifle smokes,
The animals fall down, out their blood soaks.

The bodies gone, the hunters too,
The vultures come,
They greedily enjoy their meal,
But somewhere out there a memory's real.

Memories make us what we are,
The African animals have had their share,
Of nightmares true to life,
Their horrors are not that rare.

The hunter sleeps on and dreams come to him,
Dreams much nicer than the ones he's made,
For the animals on the plains,
For the animals, the memory remains.

Lucy Crabb (13)
Devizes School

A PERFECT DREAM!

The dust of magic fairies' wings
The very first song a little bird sings
The first curl on a baby's head
The clean white sheet on an unslept-in bed
The flow of a wedding dress in the breeze
The funny sensation when you sneeze
The sparkle of a diamond ring
Newly grown daffodils in the spring
The first word you ever said
The funniest book you ever read
All the knowledge you need to know
Every bright colour of the rainbow
Remember the Christmas when we had snow
Your parents at Sports Day shouting 'Go, go, go!'
No monsters, no blood, no deaths, no screams
These are the things for a perfect dream.

Lianne Jones (11)
Devizes School

HALLOWE'EN

Tonight I will walk in the street
Wondering whom I'm going to meet
Ghosts and ghouls and scary things
Flying bats with scaly wings
Rustling bags with delicious treats
Children's faces covered in sweets
Trenching through the sloshy mud
Walking past Dracula teeth covered in blood
My face washed up bright and clear
Goodbye Hallowe'en for another year.

Carrie Wilson (11)
Greendown Community School

AUTUMN! AUTUMN! AUTUMN!

Here I am
On the tree
Dead as a dog but still alive, just.
Here comes the wind to blow me away.

Whoosh!
I'm off the branch and slowly going to my grave,
Whirling and roller-coastering down . . . down . . . down!

I see my fellow leaves
Golden, brown, emerald,
They are all different colours,
Probably each unique.

Some twirling, others swarming the streets.
I start to float down,
Then comes another gush.

Whoosh!
I'm far, far away from my only home,
Some have already landed but I'm still in the air.

Bang!
I've finally landed on the fresh green, green grass.

Mike Wilson (13)
Greendown Community School

THE FULL MOON

The full moon
The full moon,
They come out from the tomb.
They might,
They might,
They might
Come in the dead of night.
The vampires with their deadly teeth,
The monsters that eat nothing but beef.
The witches on their broomsticks ride,
They all go off side by side.
We go to trick or treating,
But everywhere the blood is leaking.
We see a ghoul with lots of bibs
Eating a chunk of a little girl's ribs
Hallowe'en, the scariest night of all.

We hear the creak of an opening door
We hear the sound of the creaky stair,
Could this really be a scary nightmare?

Nathan Barlow (11)
Greendown Community School

AUTUMN

There once was a leaf
Its colour was a golden brown
When it fell off the tree, it glided to the ground.

It swirled around on the floor not knowing where to go,
When all of a sudden, the wind came,
And the leaves began a game.

They whirled, they twirled and they cascaded.
All having lots of fun,
They stayed that way until they saw the sun!

They realised they had to leave,
It was time to say goodbye,
So they laid down, it was time to die!

Rebecca White (14)
Greendown Community School

FOOD TODAY

My great gran says I must eat pigs' feet
because you get your protein from meat.
I think my great gran is somewhat barmy,
Gran says it's from her days in the Land Army.
Grow lots of carrots so you can see,
is something she's always telling me.
My mum says 'It's the vitamins that you need,'
and to her I must pay heed.
I must eat my veg and pasta
then I can run even 'fasta'.
Cakes and sweets I can have some,
but too many make a big fat tum.
Pulses are good to give you a start,
but too many beans make you fart!
Carbohydrates come from bread,
eat lots of these or you may be dead.
The main thing in life is to eat 'healthy',
but to do this well you must be wealthy.

Sam Vaughan (12)
Greendown Community School

EATING HEALTHY

If you want to eat healthy, eat like me,
because what I like to eat is a bowl of muesli.
then I wash it down with freshly poured tea.

If it's a hot sunny day and you're getting thirsty,
remember that you must still drink healthily,
Because what I like to drink is a cup of Sunny D
In this drink is Vitamin C
So drink like me.

If you want a pudding that's healthy
have some fruit because it's nice to eat,
then wash it all down with freshly poured tea

So eat like me
And you'll be healthy.

Tanya Lowry (12)
Greendown Community School

WHEN I'M BY THE SEA

When I'm by the sea
It's all very peaceful
I can almost hear my echo
Across the rolling sands.

When I'm by the sea
It's almost like a windy day
When the waves go roaring
Across the rocky shore.

When I'm by the sea
I can sit and have a picnic
But the sea will not disturb me
Because it's all a dream.

Laura Major (12)
Greendown Community School

ALONE

Alone in the world so cruel,
asleep on the hard concrete floor.
A cold gloomy night
like yesterday and the day before.
The sun rising into the sky,
like a beachball upon the shore.
Another sparkling morning,
like yesterday and the day before.
As he walks through the streets,
begging and asking for more.
Wearing those filthy rags,
like yesterday and the day before.
Taking a bite of his sandwich,
feeling frightened and quite unsure.
Looking in bins for scraps,
like yesterday and the day before.
So many sad memories
of how it was before.
Thinking of friends and family
like yesterday and the day before.

Sneha Mehta (12)
Greendown Community School

THE ONCE CALM SEA

The shining moon shimmers on the crystal surface of the calm sea,
Whispering a soft lullaby, gently patting The Needle's cliffs.
The sea is at rest, the sea is calm.
But then! A gust of rain, a strike of lightning, transforms this once calm
sea into an all powerful monster of the night.
Roaring and crashing, to and fro faster and faster, eroding against The
Needles's cliffs.
Only one thing can stand still.
Perched on a rock against this once calm sea,
The lighthouse warns all boats to *stay away!*
As it watches the stacks of The Needle's cliffs disappearing
disappearing, disappearing
into this once calm sea.

Sandish Kaur Benning (13)
Greendown Community School

WEEPING WILLOW

Weeping willow, why dost thou weep?
Thou weepest for loss of joy.
Weeping willow why dost thou cry?
Thou cries for thy children who brighten thy skies.
Weeping willow why dost thou see tears?
Thou brings tears to chase away fears.
Why dost thou chase away fears, weeping willow?
To bring thy world its good years.
To bring thy world its good years, thou must not
cry.
Oh weeping willow we all live to die.

Jane McClintock (14)
Greendown Community School

AUTUMN LEAVES

Leaves cascade down from the trees
The children play with the colourful leaves
Green, brown, orange and yellow all together like
          an autumn rainbow
Whirling down from the trees
The tree is bare and a dingy brown
All the leaves yellow like a king and queen's crown
All the colours dancing down like a raindrop
          onto the ground.
Gliding leaves throughout the sky whirling down like
          a bird to the ground
Swirling, twirling on the grass
Autumn is here and it's leaving next year.

Emma Wakeling (13)
Greendown Community School

THE TEACHER!

T oday is the dreaded day, I'm going back to school.
H elp me, help me, what am I going to do?
E vil, evil, especially Mrs Reture, she's my teacher.

T oday is the dreaded day, I'm going back to school.
E ach moment I take a deep breath and say it's OK.
A t any moment I'll see her and she'll say 'Can't you come neater?'
C an you feel sorry for me? 'Cause I do.
H ere I am in the classroom, there's not a lot of room.
E verybody's tired except for me.
R eture the . . . the . . . the . . . teacher she's here. Oh dear what am
I going to do?

Amy Roberts (12)
Patchway High School

A HOLIDAY IN MALTA

A lways a lot of excitement as we leave.

H aving a quick bite to eat and a drink before we set off.
O ver the bridge excitement everywhere.
L eaving the car in the car park, getting ready to get on the plane.
I 'm getting everyone ready to board the plane and getting
                                                    to the gate on time.
D ad's calming Mum down and saying 'Everything's OK.'
A nd finally we're on the bus to the plane.
Y es, I'm not on my own.

I 'm by the window, yes I get a view.
N ever mind mum, you'll be OK.

M um is getting more and more worried as we go through turbulence.
A nd from above the cloud it's quite cold, but,
L ovely weather isn't it?
T owards the end of the flight, we're having a drink
A nd we've landed. It's nice and hot here.
    Mum is happy to be on solid ground.

Rebekah Smale (12)
Patchway High School

MY POEM

Perfect bimbo, that's Phoebe
Her personality is easy going, that's Phoebe
Every day
Every night she plays her guitar
Badly in the spotlight, it's
Enough to drive you crazy
Every day, every night, that's Phoebe.

Cassie de Souza (13)
Patchway High School

DRIVING LESSONS!

D riving lessons coming soon when I'm 17,
R ight now I'm only 12,
I 'll have to wait and see.
V auxhall Vectra is the car I want,
I n the garage window,
N ext thing you know I'll be on the road,
G iving lifts to friends I know,

L eaving parties later,
E ndless bus journeys no more.
S now, rain and hail, I'll be nice and warm,
S itting in my car with the heating on.
O nly drawback is the cost,
N ext week's money's always gone,
S till I'm only 12 - that's 5 years on!

Nicola Edge (12)
Patchway High School

CARS

I like cars, they're really cool
Honda, Dodge, I like them all
Flying down the motorway
In my Porsche, they all give way
Ferrari have their high speed cars
They go fast and really far
I like Chevy and Nissan
I even like Mercedes vans
McLaren have the best Formula 1 cars
Driving a Beetle is really fun
I like old Spitfires
And the new Chryslers.

Mark Giltrow (13)
Patchway High School

ANYTHING IS ANYTHING

A nything is anything
N ever been discovered
Y ellow and red big balloons
T hat's anything
H umming bees, buzz buzz buzz
I t's anything
N ever been discovered
G o on find out please

I t could be
S omething great

A nd I really want to know
N othing has been found
Y et but I might soon
T hings are rushing through my head
H aven't found a thing
I think I've got it you
N ever know
G reat I know it's anything.

Chrissie Fanson (12)
Patchway High School

AMERICA

A merica is great, Orlando is the place.
M erry and jolly, the people are always talking all the time to everyone.
E very day in the pool and in the sun is what you do.
R ides are there in Walt Disney and fairs.
I n bush gardens roller-coasters are there, you can get very sick
    on them.
C oming down the water slide, the biggest one in the world.
A merica is the best. I hope I go there again this year, that's for sure.

Danielle Martin (12)
Patchway High School

MY MOTHER

I lay upon my lovely bed,
It's time to move my sleepy head.
I hear my mother start to moan,
So I hide my head and begin to groan.
Now I hear my alarm clock tick,
It sounds so loud it makes me sick.
My mother shouts at me once more,
I can't be bothered so I ignore.
I hear on the final stair,
Oh my God she's almost there.
The door opens with a jerk,
I hide my head and begin to smirk.
The quilt's pulled back with a flick,
Still I lie there looking sick.
Trouble is mother's no fool,
No matter what, it's time for school.

Matthew Welsh (12)
Patchway High School

TEACHERS

Teachers are *never* late
and *never* swing on the school gate
or play *dares*
Don't drop food
don't wanna be a *cool dude.*
They *never* fiddle
and they make sure
that they don't *dribble.*

Joe Gibson (11)
Patchway High School

ROLLER-COASTER

In the queue I feel a judder.
Hearing the carriage go *clunk, clunk, clunk,*
Knowing that will be me in a minute.
I feel my belly lurch, then . . . *whoosh!*
The carriage returns,
Green faced people rush for their ride photos.
Alas my turn has finally come.
I sit in the seat, I clench my fists, the bars go down,
Securing you in.
I break out in a cold sweat as the carriage leaves,
As the carriage tilts it starts the agonising trek to the top,
I know there's no turning back.
I reach the top,
My heart stops as I look around . . .
Whoooosh!
I sink in the seat as I twist, turn, loop-the-loop and corkscrew
along the track.
I feel my stomach start to rumble,
My insides are all in a terrible jumble.
My lunch becomes all corrupt,
As my stomach is about to erupt!
Aaaaaagh!

Christopher Stone (12)
Patchway High School

A POSTCARD FROM DUBAI

D ust clouds swirling around in the warm wind
U ntouched lands beyond the reach of civilisation
B eaches, so long and golden, running . . .
A longside the clear blue waters of an enchanted ocean
I   t is an excursion that will never leave the memory.

Samir Jones (15)
Patchway High School

MY FAVOURITE PLACE . . . WITH MY FAMILY

W armth and love are always mine
I am at home where the sun always shines
T he people who mean the most to me are
H ere, just where I want them to be.

M y family.
Y es, they are all I need. Without them my heart would bleed.
They are my best

F riends, my incomparable friends. My desire for another family
is none, as you would see if you saw me with them.
A happy home is what I have.
M y mother is my treasure, the love of my life.
I love them. My love is so strong that even a thousand cannons
could not break my adoration for them.
L ove is at its deepest with my family.
Y ou see, they are the nicest people you'll ever meet.
My love for them is uncommonly deep.

Victoria Poole (15)
Patchway High School

RUGBY MATCH

R aining Sunday, getting psyched up!
U nder the posts waiting for the kick.
G etting ready for the kick please God make them miss.
B lasting the ball at the posts.
Y es they've missed.

G oing down the line, hoping for a try.
A re there any players?
M unched
Eager to get up, I think I broke my body!

Andrew Russell (13)
Patchway High School

BACK TO SCHOOL

My bag is packed, I'm ready to go
It's back to school and time to show
If I'm bad or if I'm good
I'm starting to think whether I should
Go to school or act very sick
That would be a very bad trick
I might be late
And then I would hate
My first day at school
Just being a fool
What am I worried about?
The teacher? No
His shout?
The smell of his breath?
The sound of his voice?
It makes me wonder what's his first choice
He could shout at you
He could shout at me
My guess is we will just have to see!

Nicola Cooper (12)
Patchway High School

MY GRAN

I love my gran, she gives me sweets and lots of treats for me to eat
I love my gran because when I sleep I stay up late and watch TV
I love my gran, she makes me cakes and takes me out, it is so great
I love my gran she wears all black
I love my gran for making my dad who met my mum, they made me
so I can say with all my heart, I love my gran.

Toby Hughes (12)
Patchway High School

THE BAR BEACH

My favourite place
The Bar Beach, awake with life
Waves - Nature's beauty.

The smell of lobsters,
Fill my nose, hmm delicious.
People sunbathing.

The taste of chicken
The taste of coconut milk
How sensational!

The sweet air. Playing
With seashells, sand all over
My feet. The sweet sand.

Boats sailing in the
sea. Tides in and out. Oh how
I love the Bar Beach.

Emma Solanke (13)
Patchway High School

A FISHY POEM

Goldfish, goldfish he looks so bored
Goldfish, goldfish you put fish flakes in the tank, he still looks bored
You buy him a friend which he just ignores
Goldfish, goldfish maybe we could buy you a TV which you will
probably ignore
Goldfish, goldfish we tap on the tank, you dart away, that's the most
interesting thing you've done all day.

Fish for tea! That sounds OK.

Luke Flicker (12)
Patchway High School

AT SCHOOL

When I'm at school
I act like a fool
I don't understand
I'm in my own wonderland

I learn what I can
And try to do what is right
Sometimes I'm wrong
Normally I am wrong
Most of the time
And that's because I like telling you poems

But wait, don't go
I need to make sure this rhyme will flow

The school is big
And lots of children go there
But let me warn you, they'll cut off your hair
That's if it's too long

No, no, no, no, no
That's my favourite joke
Let me tell you, you shouldn't smoke
But if you do
You might get a detention
It's a quite good, that they do that
You should all agree with me
But if you don't
One day you'll figure out that school
Is rather cool.

Genevieve Anniss (12)
Patchway High School

THE AIR DISPLAY

I remember my first year
The roar of jets hurting my ear
Those skilful pilots - how they flew!
Through that sky so clear and blue
The B2 Bomber so large and new
And the lines of displays - how they grew!
You see a Spitfire cut through the sky
And the fast jet pilot preparing to fly
They notice the Typhoon starting to soar
Hear the tannoy-man; He's such a bore
The kerosene smell so strong and sickly
Watch the Starfighter fly so jolly quickly
And as the day draws to a close
It's true everybody knows
So long as the jet exhaust blows
We shall return another year
Better take plugs to save my ears!

Craig Jordan (15)
Patchway High School

I LOVE BASKETBALL!

I like basketball
Even though I'm small
The feel of the ball is squishy
The smell of the court is fishy
The crowd make a lot of noise
Especially all the boys
The cheer leaders sing when you score
They want you to score loads more
Scoring is exciting
And missing a shot is quite frightening.

Karel Hartley (13)
Patchway High School

MY LOFT

My loft is a messy place it's
cluttered up with things,
All the spiders hang there dangling
from their strings!
If you go up there in the morning
you will hear the birds in song.
But if you go up there in the winter
you will need a coat on.
It is very cold up there especially in
the winter.
There is lots of wood up there, be careful
you don't get a splinter!
I used to play my keyboard up there but
there wasn't that much space.
I thought I'd better move it and find
a bigger place!

Helen Wallace (11)
Patchway High School

AUTUMN

Red and yellow crispy leaves
falling from the autumn trees.
Swiftly comes the cool wind
brushing against my soft skin.
Crunching under my feet,
the leaves fall to meet.
Frost on the leaves
glistening in the sun.
Children playing - having fun.

Rhiannon Godfrey (11)
Patchway High School

MY FAVOURITE PLACE

Pink and green wallpaper and all
of my cuddly toys,
My silver hi-fi pumping out the
Backstreet Boys.
Noisy cars passing by on the
dual carriageway.
I look outside and I can see
another sunny day.
A cascade of clouds in the sky.
I look above and all I can see
is white ceiling high.
The dog next door is running
round and round.
The children on the other side
are making lots of sound.
My little tank of water is filled
with my two fish.
My bedroom is my favourite place,
where I'm safe and warm in here.
I want to stay here . . . This is my wish.

Genna Mills (13)
Patchway High School

UNITED

U nited, united are the best you will
N ever beat them because they're just the best
I mpossible to beat never lost, I'm
T elling you they are just simply the best
E ven all of the other team will tell you they're the
D eadliest team in the Premiership.

Ben Trisic (11)
Patchway High School

MY DOG HOLLY

My dog Holly is brown and furry
She greets me every day
If a stranger comes in - she growls
To frighten them away.

Her nose is cold and wet
She sleeps in a cardboard box
Her tail is big and bushy
She looks just like a fox.

She was born at Christmastime
That's why we called her Holly.
And if I have to read this out
I won't half feel a Wally!

Matthew Owen (11)
Patchway High School

MY POEM

I went to a party last night
The games and food were alright
But when the clock struck ten
I went home again
I went to an excellent party last night
I went home at 10
And told my family
What an excellent party
It was last night and the food was delicious.
The games were fun
It was a brilliant party last night.

Lauren Harding (11)
Patchway High School

MY GUINEA PIGS

I love Monty, Nibbles too.
I love guinea pigs - how about you?
I love their coats - such silky fur.
No! They're not cats they do not purr.
Mine are silver and cream and beige
Oh yes! They live in their cage.
By the way they love their drink
but because they can't wash themselves in the sink
we have to wash them
once a month.
They love it when they're nice and cosy
comforted by their mother - Rosie!

Kirsty Yabsley (11)
Patchway High School

MY BEDROOM

My bedroom is not big, but not small
it has lovely pictures on the wall.
When people used to walk in my room
they heard no sound.
But now I've got my mini hi-fi
all they can hear is *pound, pound, pound!*
I've got teddies - big and small.
82 I've counted them all!
I like to dance in my room
I dance to Vengaboys - *boom, boom, boom!*

Samantha Tuttiett (11)
Patchway High School

My Chocolate Dream . . .

The sweet aroma of chocolate floats up my nose.
It smells delicious and it affects me from my head
to my toes,
It reminds me of that place I once set foot in.
The building,
the place where chocolate is made.
Where the people, the workers, the happy humans
make the chocolate and then get paid.
I can hear the rumbling of the machines as they slowly,
noisily work.
I get passed a sample of chocolate that tastes
as sweet as heaven.
I count the chocolate bars as they go by - 9, 10, 11.
Chocolate, cocoa, sugar - heaven; Call it what you want!
Cadbury World is my favourite place,
When I think of it . . . It brings a smile to my face.

Genna Mills (13)
Patchway High School

Fluffy - My Rabbit

I have a rabbit called Fluffy
He's cute - white and grey
and fluffy.
He hops around the garden
over the long grass.
Eating it as he goes.
He's my best friend and
I love him a lot.

Roxanne Brooks (11)
Patchway High School

THE MAGIC OF THE NIGHT . . .

As I gaze out of my window
Into the night
At the magic of the darkness
And the flickering bright lights.
To dream of being up there
As a tiny light
Though so small, magnificent in sight.
Far away we may be,
But not for long at least.
Remember the magical darkness above
That covers us whilst we sleep.
Comforting as it may be,
But can this dream last?
I only hope it does,
As tomorrow goes past.
Darkness goes by
As we all wake.
To another new day that slowly
Waits . . .

Hannah Yapp (16)
Patchway High School

ME!

Jack, Jack - is my name
I am in the Hall of Fame.
I like Tottenham - they're the best.
They can beat teams in the west.
I am cool, especially in school.
All the people think I rule.
Thanks for listening to me . . .
Now I'm going to have my tea.

Jack Davies (11)
Patchway High School

REASONS

Lots of reasons our class made up
I've got to get off school
I won the Cup.
'Miss, Miss, there's a spider above my head.
He's really hungry, he thinks I'm bread.'
'Miss, Miss, I'm the teacher's pet
I'm really sick, I need the vet.'
'Now listen up you naughty boy . . .'

'But Miss, Miss it's not a toy
2 x 4 it's just a double!
Miss, Miss - I'm not in trouble.
Miss, Miss can I eat my smarties?'
'Yes, but don't throw any parties!'

'Come on class! Win those books!'
'Yeh! But stop giving me funny looks.
All our classes ain't fun at all.'

'Bye, bye children, it's end of school.
All of the class you've got detention.
Because you weren't paying any attention.'

'But Miss, Miss it's the end of school,
I'm not doing it at all!'

Luke Estcourt (11)
Patchway High School

CINEMA

Collecting the tickets, faking your age,
or with a partner on a date.
You go in and find your seats in the dark
waiting for the film to start.
The naughty, noisy, annoying children
sitting in the corner and then the couples
on the back row, hugging and eating popcorn.
Scary films, caring films, funny and loving,
sad and bad, shocking clips.
Coke slips and goes everywhere.
Shouting at the noisy ones, acting like
the bossy ones.
Bought lots of popcorn and gets made to share.
after the film you drive your friends round the bend,
by constantly giving away the end.

Sadie Tizzard (13)
Patchway High School

ROVERS

Rovers, Rovers are the best,
especially playing teams in the west.
When the blue flames lead
the games the people cheer
and screech in my ear!
Hopefully we'll play by the Thames,
teams like Tottenham, Chelsea, West Ham too.
Instead of playing rubbish teams
like City in Division 2.

Tim Breed (11)
Patchway High School

THE FIELD

When I'm bored I hang out in the field.
In the field I like the fresh breeze that blows
against my face when I run fast.
The grass is nice and short for a game
of football.
Luke and I climb the smooth trees
to make decent dens.
The patch of long grass is a good place to hide
if we are playing a game.
The sky is blue - without a sight of clouds.
So there's lots of space for the sun to shine down on me.
It's also a spacious place to hang around with my mates.

Nicholas Hingston (12)
Patchway High School

FAIR

I was at the fair with Jack and Luke
I went on a ride and it made me puke
Then I went on the Ferris Wheel
With my old Uncle Neil.
I went on the Waltzers
And it got rid of my ulcers.
Luke went on the merry-go-round
He came back and said it was sound.
I bought some candyfloss
from my old mate Ross
We had to go so . . .
I said - No!

Stephen Iles Atkinson (11)
Patchway High School

MY FAVOURITE PLACE

My favourite place is where I'd like to be . . .
Sitting under my favourite oak tree.
To sit there and look up at the clear blue sky
And to watch the kestrels go swooping by.
Past a tall tree I can see a narrow stream,
And as the sunlight hits it, it will gleam.
In the almost silence I can hear a squirrel
Scuttling round.
Running up trees and then down on the ground.
I sit there for a while till the sun starts
To set.
The sunset looks as if the day and night have
Just met.
The pink, orange and blue looks as if they're in
Separate rows.
And the sky just seems to glow and glow

Anna Jemmison (13)
Patchway High School

MY POEM ABOUT SHALDON

We are finally here . . .
As I step out of the car I can smell
the salty air in the breeze.
The seagulls are swooping in the sky
above my head.
I hear the waves lapping upon the beach.
As I walk along the seashore I watch the
little children playing in the sand.
I am so happy to be in my favourite place.

Alex Griffee (11)
Patchway High School

MY FAVOURITE PLACE

We're going to the airport
We're going to catch a plane
When we go to Tenerife
Things are not the same.

We forget about our normal life,
And get away for the day.
The plane is taking off,
Oh hip, hip, hooray!

The food on board is expensive
But who really cares?
We're going on holiday,
We can forget about our fares.

We arrive . . . it's midnight
And the weather is quite warm.
What a great place to be.
But Dad's not happy . . .
When he gets home and finds out he's *overdrawn!*

Luke Gregory (12)
Patchway High School

MY POEM ABOUT TREES

The oaks are blowing
Trees are growing
Bark is cracking
Buds are sticking
Twigs are breaking
Roots are bumping.

Tara Lynn (11)
Patchway High School

WISHING OF MORFA BAY

I wish I was at Morfa Bay
where it is so much fun.
A chance to be with all your friends
and play out in the sun.

I wish I was at Morfa Bay
to abseil, climb and hike.
Do archery, go caving
and ride round on your bike.

I wish I was at Morfa Bay
where we stay up all night.
Girlie chats, giggling
and a monster pillow fight.

Charlotte Evans (12)
Patchway High School

PORTUGAL

The sun shines down on the sea,
A delicious ice-cream just for me!
You can't understand what the people are saying.
The boats on the water never stop swaying.
People bathing in the sun,
Children in the pool having fun.
People buying gifts for their family,
At the market there's lots to see,
There's paintings, pottery, clothes and meats,
Books and toys, bags of sweets
All the money's gone to spend
So the holiday comes to an end!

Lisa Kellett (13)
Patchway High School

MY FAVOURITE PLACES

I have many favourite places,
The *park, High Force*, the *rugby ground*,
my bedroom and *Ashton Court*.
Each has a special place inside me.
All for very different reasons.
The *park* is where I sit to chill out
Sit and think, about anything and everything.
High Force - a massive waterfall in Northumberland.
A place I will go to many times again.
A place my dad says it's the most beautiful
waterfall in England.
I can't help but agree.
The *rugby ground* is another place to chill out.
Not to think about things, but to forget them.
Watching my favourite team play is a way for me
to get out and forget everything.
My *bedroom* is where I think my own kind of meditation!
And *Ashton Court* is a complete get-away.
A place that is very different from Horfield.
A place that could be a million miles away.
The green that spreads across the whole estate,
very different from the concrete roads of Bristol.
I guess you'd call me a natural girl!
My idea of heaven being blankets of green,
sitting under a tree or walking through arches
of trees, and the scent of real air.
No pollution . . .
I guess anywhere but the streets of a modern city.

Alexandra Smolinski (14)
Patchway High School

WHO KNOWS?

It's like a blanket of fog surrounding me
Grey, damp, bleak and sombre.
Obstacles seem to be everywhere
Left, right, behind and in front.
I try and tackle each one individually,
Breaking it down, which one first - who knows?

How do I escape this nightmare?
With fear, tears, hate or depression.
Who can help me overcome this defeating horror?
Friends, brothers, sisters, mothers, fathers
How long will it last?
Days, weeks, months, years - who knows?

How will I know it's over?
Will I see the light at the end of the tunnel?
Will I feel the sharp, fresh air in my lungs again?
Will I see the bright sun through the fog?
How will I know?
Who knows?

Karen Hankinson (15)
Patchway High School

FRANCE - PARIS

France is a fantastic friendly fun place.
It was a great place to go.
It was full of people partying and having a good time.
Disneyland was brilliant - it was a great laugh.
I'd love to go back there again.
I went with my friends . . . We talked day and night.
I thought the teachers would lose their minds!

Faye Jones (13)
Patchway High School

THE FIELD

It was a windy day in the field.
I can see the grass waving side to side,
and seeing me and Nick
kicking the ball,
up and down,
slowly.
Josh was wildly running at us,
trying to push us on the luscious grass.
I could smell the flowers invaded by bees.
Nick and I - running in the breezy wind.
To taste the ice-cream.
Ice-cold, melting in the hot sun.
Hearing the whistling of the wind
and people shouting because they scored a goal.
Feel the rough leather on the ball and feel the dry mud.
That's why I like the field.

Luke Gardener (12)
Patchway High School

THE RACE

All the action on the screen,
Colours blurring your mind - whirring.
Wound up that sound!
The air is charged with tension,
Your heart beats overtime.
Your thumb shuddering ready to drop.
The light turns green!
Down drops your thumb and the screech
Of those tyres sheer delight.
The start of another virtual race
The pleasures of the PlayStation.

Rob Flitter
Patchway High School

A POSTCARD FROM PEMBROKESHIRE

P erfectly beautiful virgin land
E mpty land, near and far
M emories of relaxation, peace
B lue sea crashing against the rocks
R agged country, brave and true
O pen spaces, full of wild and untouched flowers
K indling lit on the open log fire burning in the dark
E ndless countryside
S andy beaches everywhere you turn
H ot summer days
I dyllic backdrops, wherever you go
R oasting bodies in mid-day heat
E xcitement and anticipation as a new day begins.

Tom Hill (15)
Patchway High School

NOTTING HILL CARNIVAL

Notting Hill Carnival is the place to be
See people screaming and shouting all over the streets.
Standing still - feels like you're moving around,
because the music vibrates all over the ground.
Go and stand at the top of a house,
see millions of people dancing around.
Blowing whistles adds to the noise,
everyone's there - men, women, girls and boys.

Darren Gordon (13)
Patchway High School

THE WORLD'S GREATEST PLACE

G reatest place in the world,
R eally funny and friendly.
A lways hot and sunny
N ever cold.

C rocodile parks
A musement arcades
N ice food
A water park
R eally nice people
I love Gran Canaria - it is
A very exciting place to be.

Carl Smith (12)
Patchway High School

KYNANCE COVE

I went into the sea
and jumped off the rocks
into a pool which was deep.
Then went for a snorkel and saw a seal
we looked at each other
and the seal swam off.
I told my friends and they said yeah, yeah!
Then they saw a seal's head pop up.
I told my parents and they didn't believe me
until my sister said yeah he did!
So my favourite place is Kynance Cove.

Andy Griffiths (12)
Patchway High School

ALTON TOWERS

I arrive at Alton Towers excited and happy
I look for all the scary rides - Oblivion, Ripsaw.
Black Hole, the Corkscrew and the Nemesis too.
The smell of sweet-tasting candyfloss
lingers in the air alongside the smell
of warm chips.
The whooshing of the air as you plunge down
death defying drops and twists and turns
in 360° flips.
Travelling at gut-wrenching speeds
twisting and turning this way and that.
Going upside down and turning sharp corners.
Wow! All of a sudden the roller-coaster
has finished and you rush to rejoin the queue.
Taking a break from the wilder rides.
You can take a calm spin in the tea cups
or visit the Log Ride and Swan Lake.
There's a haunted house and thousands of
roller-coasters and even water based rides.
Endless fun.
But then it's time to go.
You beg for one last ride,
on your favourite roller-coaster.
But your mum said 'No!'
Oh well! There's always next year!

Hayley Notton (14)
Patchway High School

MY FAVOURITE PLACE

My favourite place is the cinema.
Where we watch the screen light up.
The film is scary
so soon people start to scream
at things in their sight.
Popcorn's being thrown
everyone ducks their heads
whilst screaming out loud.
The film reaches a
dramatic climax and then
people hide with fear.
The film is ending
so people go home talking
about what they've seen.

Jenni Ball (15)
Patchway High School

ST DAVID'S

S urfing on gigantic waves
T hat's really exciting

D iving in deep rockpools
A nd snorkelling between the slippery rocks
V icious fish swimming by
I t makes you think that you can fly
D ays there are so great
S t David's is such a fabulous place.

Ben Osborne (12)
Patchway High School

BOSVELD

I remember my first holiday in the Bosveld.
Memories bright, bright like the sunlight that shines
over upon the immense open fields.
Trees obscure the view of buffaloes and springboks
strolling in the distance.
An aroma of nature, the freshness of the air
and the dust after an early afternoon rain:
An aroma indescribable to anybody else.
Overjoyed people from all over the world,
near and far, no matter where you're from.
The only sound you hear is the sounds of nature.
The beauty of nature surrounds you with joy and comfort
I just can't wait to return to such beauty.

Willem Matthys Van Der Colff
Patchway High School

THE HOLIDAY IN IBIZA

The amazing place to go on holiday is Ibiza
This crazy tropical island is irresistible.
When you cross the crystal clear water
Sitting on the beach with a juicy cocktail
Sand blowing across the shore
I see the shelly shells being washed up on the beach.
Just the sun
In the sky - no clouds at all
I long to be there.

Jason Payne (12)
Patchway High School

HIDEAWAY

As I sit in school
My mind is miles away.
In the place I love the most
The place I'd like to stay.

A place that's filled with comfort
After a long day,
A place that's warm and cosy,
My little hideaway.

My hamster comes to greet me
In a place I call my own.
There's no one else to talk to
As I sit alone.

As the sun goes down
I close the curtains on the busy world outside.
I light my candles and drift away,
As I cuddle up and hide.

This is where I want to be
In my little hideaway.
Safe and sound . . .
At the end of the day.

Rachel Hextall (14)
Patchway High School

MY FAVOURITE PLACE

My favourite place
is Switzerland. I love the
quiet rolling hills.

I love the village
as people rush by shopping
early in the day.

The sun beats down on
the people walking along
drinking fresh water.

I love waterfalls
crashing down the mountain side
then flowing away.

I love the night-time
and the stars over the mountains
everything is still.

In my dreams I hope
I will soon return back there
and see it again.

Julia Postlethwaite (15)
Patchway High School

BOSTON

I can taste the salty sea air in my dry mouth
I look hungrily towards the south
I turn around and see a diner
I want to try a forty-niner
Tree-lined roads lie ahead of me
As well as lots of things to see
I'd like to travel the whole world-wide
Here in Boston cultures collide
Down the street I walk along
I glance at my ticket
I've been here too long
Oh no! It's time to go
Just as it's about to snow!

Eleanor Armstrong (14)
Patchway High School

THE WORLD OF THE PLONKY WELLICLE

Silly chang-ching-pings
eat many chick-wings.
Do a ping-pong-poo,
at about half-past two.
They say 'Willa Wawalla'
You owe me a dollar,
from when we went to Ming
bought a diddly-donkey-ding.'
Do you understand chang-ching-pings?
When they do a fang-wang-fling!
At the bottom of the scumble-jellicle,
When you go to the world of the Plonky Wellicle.'

Nikki Claire Cross (16)
Patchway High School

HOLIDAYS

The soft sand fills the print of my foot
As I walk down to the sea
With the sea breeze whistling from behind me,
The white waves smash the rocky cliffs
And the colours of the rainbow shine.
Through the bright light of the sun
The strong tidal waves pull me under
Until I feel the cold no more.
I am back at the chip shop
Enjoying a hot cup of tea, just for me.
As I write some more postcards of those happy days.

John Andrews (16)
Patchway High School

MY ROOM

I love my room
It's the best place in the world.
My PlayStation controller
Sprawled out on the floor.
Music playing at full blast
And Mum screaming to turn it down.
My cat's asleep next to the radiator.
The trees swaying from side to side in the gentle breeze.
I love my room
It's the best place in the world.

Daniel Butcher (12)
Patchway High School

A POSTCARD FROM . . .

O ld and new enjoy the fun
R esting at night for the long day to come
L ong days in the theme parks
A nd go after two weeks and leave no marks
N oisy streets are far away
D o nothing else but eat and play
O h what a great place!

John Gillard (15)
Patchway High School

TEARS RUN DRY

Knock and no voice will answer you, for I am not home.
A place of calm waters and filtered light is my secluded world.
I can see only peace and tranquillity, can hear only soft gentle tone,
shut off is the life outside from this place, to call my own.
Clouds are billowing, blobs of white, doves and nightingales fly,
I sit here feeling in harmony as the rest of the existence goes by.
My sphere is a perfect image the good made from the bad in the burning
words from the heat of a fight I sink into my power.
Blocking the screaming and changing the tears to droplets of dew
on lush grass.
Colours are fresh and cordite the sky a deep washed brass.
Do not fear for me, for only now I am happy when outside
I cannot handle I sink inside my lullaby land.
Do not weep for me, for only it is true there is no one to hate,
no one to love.
No hurt, no pain, no you!

Kate Owen (14)
Prior Park College

MOTHERHOOD

On a cold morning,
When I hear that little cry,
I go in and see him there,
Glowing like a pot of gold.

Every night it cries for attention,
I lumber out of bed.
Just to bounce and rock him on my knee,
All day he needs a cuddle.

As I see him there,
I wonder why this hell has come upon me.
A night of stupidity for this,
This little thing lying there so helpless.

The dark nights seem to last forever,
This evil dawning on me,
Trapping me for an age of life.

The thrill to kill
The wretched thing.
It's always crying and making a noise
I don't want or need him.

In a spurt of anger,
I shake him furiously,
There's no more crying, just silence.

He doesn't shine any more
He's a statue,
His movements are only in my mind.

James Andrews (14)
Prior Park College

BLOOD

I fall from the high four-legged chair,
As when my head hits the radiator.
Laughing as I see pain
Thinking of the avalanche of blood
Thick or creamy I cannot tell
The huge scar like a scrape from a paper cut
The strong music of a rampage
As the blood trickles down my blonde hair
Congratulations to the men in red!
Running out over the round hills of thick grass
Picking myself up like a cow in the field
Moaning and groaning like an elephant in despair
As I get closer to the door shouting for help
Will someone help me?
The biggest cut I have ever had, deeper than a cliff itself.
As more blood explodes out like a volcano erupting
My face whiter than ever like a sheet of snow in the Arctic -
Losing blood, heart stop pumping
Stop!
Bad boy.

Sebastian Price (13)
Prior Park College

HYPHENATED SUMMER

And I find myself . . .
Running shadow-struck across a sun-shot lawn
Past the cobwebbed dim of a rusty swing
Into a green sun-dappled tent of fairy shade
Swept with gnat-sung dreams
Resting on the broad flaked nakedness
Of a creaking green branch
And leaning into the tendrilled incense of rust-burnt leaves

And I find myself . . .
Stooping under the lichened bark and through the fan-flapping fingers
Into a sundial round of grass mown into a thumb-print swirl
And striped with ivied apple-trees
Releasing bitter-soft terracotta fruit
Surrounded and iridescent with bluebells silent in
waving-wild grasses
Primrose-flanked I fling my joyful head
Up at an explosion of friendly leaves
In a milky, cornflower-blue sky, hung with a sliver of moon
And swept with soft dreams of cloud
Past birthday-candles of budding blossom batted
alongside the crumbling wall
To a seaweed gnarled log, dryad shaped
And spider-still clutched to the bosom of the grassy earth
with a matted Lincoln wave
Peeping into overgrown, wild-flower shade
And I find myself . . .
Staring into Jabberwocky galloping branches
Bark-snaked to the awesome Warlock trunk
And scattered with a jolt as I sweep out and under and through
Into perfumed summer.

Lucinda E Peters (13)
Prior Park College

I'll Be . . .

Will anyone ever find me, care to delve into my soul's crevasses.
Care to touch my skin and note the heat and texture.
Care to smooth my hair and understand each strand of colour.
Open the eyes of a blind man and the things he has touched
will have new meaning.
Like a man with no sight, teach me, govern your eyes by your heart.
May your hands know my person, like a ship that sails its waters.
May your heart beat in time with my own.
The rhythm of clocks beating time.
A lifetime of connection . . .
Love me with your arms lifting me
Let me reach the heavens
Care to send me to Heaven.

Susan Mary Ramshaw (14)
Prior Park College

RIP

I trudged stealthily through the submerging heath
Mist hung ankle high as it engulfed my feet.
Treading tentatively along the thawing green
Willowed waters gave a ghostly sheen.
Spiderwebs embellished with diamonds of dew
The gravestones themselves a mournful blue.
In the west the sky has a rosy glow
My spirits lift - not far to go . . .
And as I head towards the light,
My heart beats faster at the sight,
Of home, it's waiting there for me,
But this journey's an eternity.
At last, I leave the hallowed ground,
I'm home, doors locked - I'm safe and sound.

Joe Richards (14)
Prior Park College

DYING TO LIVE

A girl was born her name not known,
with the strength to achieve her dreams,
an ordinary girl with normality, sensibility or so it seems.
Her aim was to get to the top, her goal was to learn how to fly,
a life of glamour in spotlight was not going to pass her by.
With her hands she clutched for stardom a chance to set herself free,
a knowing pain in the pit of her screaming life your fantasy.
With her fine boned face and well crafted frame,
she plunged her person into a life of fame,
a part of her she now had lost,
for the chance to be loved whatever the cost.
Publicity in gold glitter dressed were meant to happiness
and ego caresses,
but movie town Hollywood is not as portrayed the life of an actress
is not well paid.
Sex, drugs and rock 'n' roll was a way to bear the anguish,
of the blonde babe bombshell's striving need to sustain
her lifetime's wish.
The thing she loved the most was the thing that took her soul
she killed herself because of a life played in a role,
the thing she loved the most was the thing that held her low,
this is the tragedy Shakespeare did not write, the tale of M Monroe.

Jessica Garnet (14)
Prior Park College

PICTURE PERFECT

Shattered glass,
Distorted image,
Broken into pieces.
My face, a picture,
Broken and torn,
Separated into jagged forms.
Deadly white,
My lips blood red.
Eyes cold as steel,
And scared.
Then I'm falling,
Into a trap of insanity,
The cold wind blows,
And I'm going down,
Into emptiness.
Lost, trapped,
Pulled further from life.
Gone forever are my fears,
Pain and regrets,
Until I awake again,
And life is still,
Frozen in time.

Samantha Lodge (14)
Prior Park College

THE DAY THE DINOSAURS CAME TO TOWN

Sixty million years ago
In the late Jurassic
The Allosaurus ruled the Earth
Carnivorous and satanic.
The savage beast originated
From western USA
And no one knew where he had gone
Until 4 o'clock today.
Downtown Seattle, mid-afternoon
The rush hour reached its peak.
Suddenly and without warning
Some hills rose from the street.
The savage beasts rose to their feet
And gave triumphant roars
That toppled cars, smashed windows
Wrecked a chopper from channel four.
With piercing teeth and razor claws
Our friends took to the town.
The screaming people who ran in vain
Began to be mown down.
Little Jim was doing shopping
With his sister Joan
They stopped to buy fresh doughnuts
And never made it home.
The dinosaurs, once they were full
Crawled back into the ground
And no one knows just when or where
The next ones will be found.

Michael Please (15)
Prior Park College

LIKE A ROSE

My grandma is like a rose
Each day a petal is shed
Each night a bud is opened.
Though we do not realise
The beauty of this flower
It breathes between our hearts
And grows closer each second of every day.
So cherish each moment
That you spend with your dear rose
For one day the petals may shed
And the buds will not open.
The thorns may seem deleterious.
The petals perished
But the fragrance still lingers
In an unsurpassable way.

Emily Bradshaw (13)
Prior Park College

EVANSCENCE

I thought I knew a man
His silhouette fragile and willowy
Disappeared into an abyss
Forever and eternity.
As easy to be betrayed -
As to betray is easy,
I thought I knew a man
But did the man know me?

Sophie Jennings (16)
Prior Park College

MILLENNIUM

Year 2000 is approaching,
And some are very scared.
Worrying about what might happen,
When normally they wouldn't have cared.

People are excited,
And jumping all about.
But for me it's another excuse,
To get drunk
To scream
To shout.

Beggars line the streets
Hunger lurks around.
Pollution in the air,
Poison on the ground.
The oil is getting scarce,
The coal is running out.
If we don't stop this rape and sin
The millennium won't mean nowt!

Philip Naidoo (15)
Prior Park College

OVER THE TOP

We walk towards the enemy
fixed bayonets in our hands
men fall either side of me
from the machine gun fire.
I think of the old lie
Dulce et decorum est pro patria mori.

Daniel Whiskin (13)
The John Bentley School

TOGETHER FOREVER

See the world through the eyes of a child
See the terror, through all he's been
Yet still filled with innocence
They see a world filled with violence
Of men shooting men, of slaughtered children and women
And they wonder when people will finally see sense
They see the savageness in the eyes of the soldiers,
And the bloodshed along the roads
They pray for courage and for help
For peace and love
For an end to the conflict
And for the flight of the white dove
There is light in the shadows and shadow in light
And black in the blue of the sky
But there is still hope, for out of the desert a flower blooms
They wonder when the world will finally be at peace
Of when the lands can sing with joyous harmony
And of when we will stand united
Together forever.

Sharon Skelhorn (13)
The John Bentley School

LOVE CONFLICTS

Love is sweet
Love is kind
Love is pure
And it makes you blind

Happy as can be
Because you're in love
You could fly as
You have the wings of a dove

Then it turns cold
Your heart to stone
You've been sold
And are all alone

The conflict begins
Nowhere to go
Who will win?
Me or the foe.

Louise Jones (13)
The John Bentley School

MILLENNIUM

'What's all this fuss?' I asked my mum
'About the new millennium.'

This is what she had to say,
'The year 2000 is on its way,'

A lot has happened over a thousand years,
Some things have brought smiles and others tears,

Lots of wars with many faces,
Hospitals are growing, with more and more cases.

Neil Armstrong was the first man in space,
Henry Ford's car won the first race,

Leonardo's fame came through his art,
Whilst Clarke had a transplant of the heart.

Flemming made medicine out of mould,
Shakespeare wrote plays that he told.

Then I asked her about this 'Bug',
But she just smiled and gave a shrug.

Gemma Louise Dixon (12)
The John Bentley School

THE MILLENNIUM

The millennium is a fresh new start
I'm sure this century has made its mark.
With wars and fights along the way
We've also had our share of good days.
You hear of teenagers pulled off the street
Abused and raped it's not very neat.
Their lives have plunged in a deep deep hole
Their insecurity has taken its toll.
With a bit more precaution and safety each day
This world could be a much better place.
When things are going good each day
They're going much better than you say.
You take things for granted the way that you walk
The way that you see and the way that you talk.
We should be grateful for each day we're here
Every day, every month, every week, every year.
Let's hope as the new millennium dawns
We act better and not forlorn.
Let's make this millennium completely unique
Let's join together and not have to seek
To find peace, happiness, laughter and joy
Let's get together and make this great ploy.

Stacey Andrews (13)
The John Bentley School

BURGERS IN A BAP

Burgers in a bap, burgers in a bap,
Tall ones, short ones and some are fat,
You get them in the restaurants, you get them in the streets,
And yum, yum, yum, yum they're awfully nice to eat!

Burgers in a bap, burgers in a bap,
Tall ones, short ones and some are flat,
You can eat them in your bedroom, you can eat them in the trees,
But do one little favour, save one for me!

Lauren Murray (13)
The John Bentley School

KETCHUP CONFLICT

Mother has called you, it is time for your dinner.
'You've got to eat!' she says, 'You can't get any thinner!'
But lucky for you, tonight is the best
Pizza and chips! They beat all the rest!
So you have washed your hands, and sat down for tea
And a conflict arises, not with mother or the family.

But with the ketchup. It doesn't mean to be rude.
But let's face it! Without ketchup where's the taste in food?
So you go to open the bottle, and there is that gunk all over the lid
And did it go all over your hands? You bet it did!
By the time you have cleaned off all the mess, the food is half-cold
Now to get the ketchup out, but where on the bottle to hold?

Most people go for the neck and base, but you should see
the frustration on their face!
Others prefer to smash it to bits, they like to use a hammer
Unfortunately that counts as malicious attack, you can be put
in the slammer!
I've got a suggestion, try it *please!*
Next time buy an 'easy pour', and give it a squeeze!

Thomas Moore (13)
The John Bentley School

TWILIGHT SKY

I look beyond my garden gate,
On this summer's day so late.

A shining star,
I see afar.

The setting sun,
The only place to run.

The twilight sky,
Gives out a sigh.

At the blanket of blue,
With its misty hue.

The moon starts to lift,
For another long shift.

In the sky a pale disc,
A perfect setting, a lover's tryst.

The nightingale sings her song of grace,
The spider weaves his web of lace.

Slowly trickles the babbling river,
And the wind blows the leaves from hither to thither.

The owl that hunts when darkness falls,
The breeze that brings the vixen's calls.

But soon the sun will rise,
For all those who were wise.

And again the world will revolve,
Whilst there are problems to be solved.

Lynsey Crerar (13)
The John Bentley School

THE SEASIDE

The waves are salty and the sea is cold,
Everyone can swim from young to old.

I like surfboards, flippers, floats,
I must swim fast to avoid the boats.

When I'm swimming in the sea,
Crabs are the last thing I want to see.

When it's cold a wetsuit takes away the chill,
Did you know jellyfish can kill?

Stormy nights bring seaweed on the shore,
Also jellyfish so my mum doesn't swim any more.

I grab my boogyboard when the waves get high,
Sometimes I think I'm really going to fly.

I like rock pools, I'll take my bucket and spade,
'Hey Dad do you like the castle I've made.'

Gosh I'm really hungry, what's Mum got to eat,
Ice-cream, cakes and Pringles for a treat.

After a rest I'm back in the sea,
Don't you wish you were swimming here with me?

Katie Levy (12)
The John Bentley School

'TIS A RABBIT GOOD AND STRONG

On a spike, the puppy lies
One hundred thousand fleas did cry
Then Filbert came along
'Tis a rabbit good and strong

He carries with him a battle-axe
The ropes of oppression that he hacks
The bells in the church go ding-dong
'Tis a rabbit good and strong

When the cows go moo
And the ghosts go boo
You can smell the pong
'Tis a rabbit good and strong

Filbert saw an aardvark's arse
Which was implanted onto glass
His arms were particularly long
'Tis a rabbit good and strong

I like cabbage.

Richard Coward (13)
The John Bentley School

THE SPECIAL PERSON

You can't buy love,
It doesn't grow on trees,
But when that special person comes,
You certainly feel it,

You can't see love,
You can't draw it either,
But when that special person comes,
You definitely feel it.

Love doesn't come in spray cans,
You won't find it in shops,
But when that special person comes,
You definitely feel it.

Where there's love there's conflict,
Conflict equals arguments,
But when that special person goes,
You still feel it . . .

Rob Taylor (13)
The John Bentley School

LOVE AND CONFLICT

L ove is also warmth,
O r admiration and adoration.
V ery likely in your life, love for another will
E dge near.

A nd as for conflict,
N ot a nice thing,
D o not go near it just have a laugh.

C onflict is to fight or disagree,
O r shout at one another, friends and family.
N o person likes to do it
F or it is horrible, but in the end it'll never change,
L ove
I s different to
C onflict,
T ry not to argue, or you'll get the stick.

Samantha Brazell (13)
The John Bentley School

LOVE AND CONFLICT

Love is a gift from heaven
Conflict is a curse from hell
But it takes mankind to bring them
To this world we all love so well

We take care of our families and friends
And always consider their feelings
We're ready to make amends
When we've upset them by our dealings

But when strangers have different ideas
Their beliefs can make us feel threatened
There can be doubts, mistrust and fears
And we react to insults unmentioned

And so from just simple misjudgements
A conflict can flare and explode
Instead of trust and involvement
There is anger, distance and cold

But hopefully we all understand
That love will always be pure
And even if built on sand
Is still worth the effort, I'm sure.

Claudie Fenwick (13)
The John Bentley School

ROMEO AND JULIET'S LOVE

R omance
O dyssey
M agnificent
E nchanted
O bsessions

A tmospheric
N ightmare
D ashing

J udicious
U nlucky
L ove story
I ncredible
E dging
T ragedy.

Samantha Craddock & Keeley Carter (12)
The John Bentley School

MOONLIGHT

M oonlight means love over a candlelight dinner
O ccasionally the candles would flicker from the sea breeze
O ccupying each other's thoughts constantly
N ever being distracted by the breaking waves on the beach
L ove is floating around the dimly lit room
I n the room it was heating up minute by minute second by second
G leaming rays from the moon reflecting on the calm ocean waves
H ere eyes looked like diamonds sparkling in the light
T hen we would move to the bedroom for desert.

David Holmes (15)
The John Bentley School

WHY

(In loving memory of Simon Hawkins age 8)

You don't understand
Because you're not alone.
You are complete,
I am alone.
You can't see my anger,
You can't feel my pain.
My brother was here yesterday,
Today he is not.

The pain of not seeing him
Is like a thousand knives stabbing me all over.
I can't stop the bleeding,
I can't control the pain.
I am the one in pain,
Just me, no one else.

Not knowing what to do,
Not knowing the answer why.
I am asking myself what he did wrong?
I will never know the answer,
A good job too, I cry.
I want to see my brother,
But no one can help me.
Why?

Christopher Hawkins (15)
The John Bentley School

NATURAL PHENOMENON - WATER

Trickling beauty
Over the smooth stones of its path.
Dawdling flow in the rhythm of nature
Until the rain falls.
Drip, plop.
Trickling no more.
It's a rushing torrent of anger
Rushing for its goal, wherever it is.
Waterfall over its hellish drop
Until it calms
A trickling beauty once more.

Rachael Gardner-Stephens (12)
The John Bentley School

POSSESSIONS

My box is red and white,
Chequered, a tablecloth pattern,
Card and plastic, chalk and cheese,
Eight inches by five inches, small and simple.

Inside my box are six,
Nay seven! (as there is one free),
'Mini bakewell tarts', each
With half a glace cherry, sunbathing on top.

This box is a dead loss,
Nothing important lies within,
Just food (and sugary food at that)
But still, my food in my red box.

Peter Blackstock (12)
Wells Cathedral School

A CASKET FULL OF SECRETS

Shall I tell you a secret?
It involves your trust,
It is about the brown casket that I found,
I found it on my way home from school,
It just sat in the puddle, the lock's rusty,
So I took it home.
I did not tell my family,
I wanted it to be a secret,
I was thinking about opening it,
However then it would not be a secret,
So it stays in my room,
And every night when nobody is near,
Then is the only time I can see
The secrets spill out in a sparkling gold powder,
It fills my ears and my dreams,
And I sleep soundly,
Content with myself,
The secrets, they sleep,
Those secrets which will never be told,
And that golden key,
That locks the secrets away,
In the casket and in my heart,
And in my heart they will stay,
Just like they do in the brown casket,
That locks away the secrets.

Anna de Lacey (12)
Wells Cathedral School

THE LIGHTHOUSE

Standing tall and slim against the night sky,
Its beacon flashing yellow,
Warning sailors of the peril nearby.
The cold grey jagged rocks beneath,
With sea lashing up to them will cause so much grief.
If only people knew what horrors you hold,
In these rocks so large and cold,
Ghostly voices from the ships that smashed,
As onto the rocks they have crashed.
So innocent looking that beach nearby,
Where children play but sailors die.
Lighthouse lighthouse keep flashing do,
For the sailors' lives depend upon you.

Richard Bevan (12)
Wells Cathedral School

WHY?

Everyone in school wants commendations, why?
Everyone has presents at Christmas, why?
Everyone has things that they like or dislike, why?
Everyone was a baby or a child, why?
Everyone will be a woman or a man, why?

Girls play hockey and boys play rugby, why?
I always want to ask 'Why?' why?
But I really don't know why, why?
Don't ask me 'Why?' why?
Because I - don't - know - why!

Harmonee Tsang (13)
Wells Cathedral School

THE LIGHTHOUSE

The lighthouse stands,
alone,
out on the rock,
protruding from the waves,
that hold, danger.

The light shines,
out,
over the waves,
and tells all,
to be wary.

Out over the water,
warning,
to the ships,
about the rocks,
waiting, for the kill.

With great importance,
it shines,
and shows all,
the way to go.
The lighthouse, stands.

William Brown (12)
Wells Cathedral School

THE CASKETS

The three caskets sit in silent splendour,
Behind the silken curtain,
The fates of many they will decide.

The first is gold, all glistening and shining
The second is silver, so very noble and proud
The last is lead, all dull and grey.

The golden chest is bright and carved
Some said gold was love,
And carrion did they find.

The silver box glistens in the light
But love it did not have
Instead just empty to all who search

The lead case is so dull it soaks the light
And love it shall contain
For those who can stoop beyond their pride for love
Shall get the hand in marriage.

Tom Laws (12)
Wells Cathedral School

I AM MYSELF!

Our marriage was most like a boat,
Which first sailed smoothly in a hopeful breeze,
But soon a never-ending storm,
Then pushed us into pointless seas.

And now be-calmed, alone,
I view the ocean of my life.
I am the captain of my fate,
I am myself! Not just a wife.

Eleanor Scrivens (14)
Wootton Bassett School

FOREVER FREE

Black plumage as deep and black
As the shadow within its heart,
A raven.
Its sharp eyes,
Always alert.
It will kill its own if hungry.

As it soars the skies
It is forever alert.
Down below is its prey,
Cowering if the raven comes near.
If its shadow passes,
A fear will rise within you.

An eternal hate fills its heart,
Unable to care.
Its mate lasts one year,
And one year only.
Then he takes to the skies,
Forever free.

Laura Merry (14)
Wootton Bassett School

LEAVING SCHOOL

It's been a busy year
For the year sixes here
And they think it's really cool
That they're leaving primary school

They'll go up into year seven
Right up to year eleven
Having lots of fun
But missing everyone

This is a very sad day
For it is their last day
So there's just one last thing to be said
And that thing is 'Goodbye.'

Lorraine Newton (11)
Wootton Bassett School

EQUAL!

When I look out of my home
I see people without a home
Why do they have no home?

When I put on my clothes
I see people with ragged clothes.
Why do they have ragged clothes?

When I have my dinner
I think of people starving
Why do they have no dinner?

When I think of my parents
I see people without parents
Why are they abandoned?

When I go to school
I pass people with no education
Why don't they go to school?

When I buy something with my money
I pass people without any money
Why do people have no money?

I wish everybody was
Equal!

Sophie Wallace (11)
Wootton Bassett School

It Feels Titanic

At the start it's great.
You're travelling in waters you've never travelled in before.

You get closer and closer.
Then it hits you.
Like an iceberg.

You didn't see it at first.
But then you start to notice.

You thought you were unsinkable.
Until you sunk.
Down into a world of darkness.
Down and down you go.

You try to pick up.
Then you hit the rock bottom.

Your shell is cracked.
Your body is crushed.
Your engine is burnt out.

Is there no *escape?*

Shane McAteer (14)
Wootton Bassett School

Conkers

Today I was found on the floor
I was picked up
I got two ears
With a bit of rope in the holes.

I play my friend
I swing *I miss* they swing I am hurt
They swing again I am smashed
I am no *more.*

Karl Brant (12)
Wootton Bassett School

THE WHOLE TOWN IS SLEEPING

The lonely one.
He strikes again.
I don't know why.
I don't know when.
They found Eliza
In a bush.
Dead, dead.
He killed her stone dead.
Now he is gone.

The lonely one
He strikes again.
Lavinia was scared.
Lavinia turns around
And the story ends.
Can you guess what happened to
Lavinia Nebbs . . . ?

The whole town's sleeping
But not for long
Because the screams of Lavinia
Could be deafening.

Laina Stephens (15)
Wootton Bassett School

IS THERE LIFE OUT THERE?

Often I sit down at night,
And look up at the stars.
I wonder 'Is there life out there,
On Mercury or Mars?'

Do strange creatures float round up there,
Squinting through the black.
Do they ever realise that,
We're down here looking back.

If I could build a rocket,
I'd fly up there and round.
Then I'd rush back down again,
To write down what I'd found.

But what would I have found up there,
Once I'd got up at last?
Would I have found the future,
Or maybe the past?

What colour would the landscape be,
Green or even blue.
Red or yellow, grey or black,
Or white and purple too?

Would people there be friendly,
Just like me or you.
Or would they be our enemy,
And hate us through and through.

Often I sit down at night,
And look up to the stars.
And now I know that there is life,
On Mercury and Mars.

Kirsty Stuyvesant (11)
Wootton Bassett School

THE VILLAGE AND ITS WIND

The wind is cool,
Cool as a breeze,
A gentle whisper calling,
Right through the trees.

All is fast,
Angry and strong,
The terrible storm which
Lasts awfully long.

Now all is quiet,
Peaceful and still,
The tornado has gone,
And the village looks ill.

The wind is now playful,
At the highest of heights,
Where it is tossing,
All of the kites.

The soft and happy gale,
That is warm not cold,
Is gentle and kind,
But does not do what it is told.

The harsh sting,
Of the spiteful whip,
That hurts the face,
Or the quivering lip.

The autumn leaves, with
The wind they swiftly float,
Across the pond,
Like a free spirited boat.

Laura Aitkenhead (12)
Wootton Bassett School

POEM

In the glistening moonlight,
The dreary dog walking slowly,
Tired and lonely,
Run away from home,
Sleep is just a dream,
Food is just a whisper,
As the dog lays down in silence,
To sleep quietly at rest,
The dawn rises across the sky,
Full of cheerful joy,
But then sad and lonely
The dog awakes
To an oncoming car,
Heading straight for him
He doesn't have the energy to move
Closer - Closer - *splat!*

Naomi Ball (12)
Wootton Bassett School

CONKERS

As I hang among the army of green silken spears,
I see my kind fall from the sky to their frightening doom.
Our shells sharp as razors slice through the twigs as we travel down,
Our piercing protection will not save us yet,
For the children will get through to our smooth brown gold.
Soon it will be my turn.
Then I start to fall,
I hit the earth,
My body splits,
I can only hope I blend in with the ground.

Chris Gallimore (12)
Wootton Bassett School

WINTER

Children sleighing down a hill,
While the snowman stands so still.

Snowballs flying through the air,
Brushing through my cold wet hair.

Snow is falling on the trees,
Gently swaying with a breeze.

Snow is falling down, down, down,
Falling down upon our town.

It's snowing now hip, hip hooray,
Come on kids let's go and play.

Hip, hip hooray it's starting to snow,
Come on you lot, here we go.

Snowmen standing up so straight,
One is right inside my gate.

Snowmen standing up so tall,
Watch out here comes a *big* snowball.

Snow so soft is such a sight,
Upon this beautiful starry night.

As I'm rushing down the path,
I'm dreaming of a nice hot bath.

Light and crispy under feet,
What a cold and lovely treat.

I want to get home out of the breeze,
Because out here I'm going to freeze.

Samantha Prictor (11)
Wootton Bassett School

THE SEASIDE

The golden sand
The deep blue sea
The scorching sun
A pier like a never-ending ruler

The polished pebbles
The bombarding seagulls
The light blue sky
A crab like a spider scuttling along the sand

The smiling faces
The sailing ships
The screaming children
I have been to the seaside.

Naomi Strange (11)
Wootton Bassett School

BAD NEWS

It was ten o'clock when
We got the bad news.
Gran had died.
She had a heart attack.
I was sat next to Mum
When they told her.
Her eyes filled with tears.
Her face was all hot and red.
Her life had been torn apart
By the bad news.
Nothing would be the same again.
I was devastated,
So was Mum.

Kelly Bowers (14)
Wootton Bassett School

I WAS STRANDED!

I was stranded on an island,
I didn't know where I was,
I didn't know how I got here,
But I wish I was at home.
I went on the beach,
The waves blast against the rocks.
You could hear the sea roar when it hits the rocks.
I wish I was at home so then I could snuggle up in bed.
The palm trees all great and big,
Hides away the sun.
The seagulls squawk when they go over the rocks
And dive when they see food.
The wind howls in my ear
What makes me get all scared,
But I wish I was at home.

Taryn Fearnley (15)
Wootton Bassett School

POUND

All I had was a single pound
It was the first I'd ever found
I found it so many years ago
The day we had all that snow.

I stopped and stared and had a look
I went home and got my bank book.

All I had was 99 pounds including that
One I found and now I have 100 pounds
And I am so proud

And now I have 100 pounds including the one I found.

Sam Burchell (14)
Wootton Bassett School

THE TALE OF TERROR

The lunatic comes again
And casts his eyes on a kind gentleman
He travels up
And travels down
He travels around in a balloon
To enjoy the view

The lunatic comes again
But this time he starts to talk
The gentleman was very scared
He didn't know what to say
Till a voice said 'Do you have any children?'

The lunatic comes again
But this time to kill the kind gentleman
All he did was creep up
And throw his arms around his body.

Zoë Stewart (15)
Wootton Bassett School

PHOTO ALBUM

Empty eyes stare out from the portraits,
As they have for many years,
A swaying ocean of memories,
Of joy and life and tears.

A bright eyed girl and her grandma,
Standing, smiles on faces,
Dust lies on the faded prints,
Of the dearest of people and places.

Those once so close to the heart,
Forgotten places found,
All live on in photographs,
But do not make a sound.

A precious book of family,
Important more than any,
The most valuable possession,
That isn't worth a penny.

Bethan Staton (11)
Wootton Bassett School

MY LIST POEM

I like football,
 I hate school.
  I like roller-blades,
   I hate spades.
    I like computers,
     I hate scooters.
      I like the link,
       I hate pink.
    I like blisters,
I hate sisters.
  I like speeding,
   I hate reading.
     I like biking,
      I hate writing.
        I like the rain,
         But I'm not insane.

Adam Masters (14)
Wootton Bassett School

THE SINGING ZOO

Squirrel, squirrel,
Shake your bushy tail,
Squirrel, squirrel,
Shake your bushy tail,
Put your nuts between your toes,
Crinkle up your little nose,
Squirrel, squirrel,
Shake your bushy tail.

Elephant, elephant,
Clomp your great big feet,
Elephant, elephant,
Clomp your great big feet,
Crush up all your monkey nuts,
Stand on all the rabbit huts,
Elephant, elephant,
Clomp your great big feet.

Monkey, monkey,
Swing your long, long arms,
Monkey, monkey,
Swing your long, long arms,
Use your tail to hold on tight,
Never ever start a fight,
Monkey, monkey,
Swing your long, long arms.

Samantha Hayward (11)
Wootton Bassett School

WATER

It trickles down my windowpane,
Droplets of nature's water,
It's beautiful and transparent,
Shame it ends up down the drain.

It keeps us alive and part of the world,
Recycled and reused,
It's some people's saviour,
Unfortunately there isn't enough to go
round the world.

It falls from the open heavens above,
And is in reservoirs,
It's pulled up from the wells,
It's water. It covers 70% of the world.

Nicola Foster (11)
Wootton Bassett School

MY DOG BOB

Bob my dog is never white.
He never barks all through the night.
He likes to go on a long walk.
It would be great if he could talk.

His favourite toy is his ball.
I do not think he's very tall.
I really love him very much.
Because he's got that secret touch.

Kirsty Swan (11)
Wootton Bassett School

Missile Command

On cold sea we be
Sailing to freedom on the cold sea
Till the sunrise of the north come be.

Then fast and silent they come
Bang! Bang! Bang! Bang! Bang!
That was then.

This is now
Guy Fawkes Night 1999
And again fire burns in hatred
The memory glows for years to come
But still I be a sombre man.

Nicholas Oliver (12)
Wootton Bassett School

Cuckoo

I am a cuckoo
I cuckoo at twelve
Sitting in a box
Waiting till 12.00
It's 9.00 now four hours to go
9.00, 10, 11, 12. It's time
for me to chime
Cuckoo cuckoo
I have done my thing
I just have to wait again.

Elizabeth Dickson (12)
Wootton Bassett School

ON THE DUSTY SHELF

When I was first bought
everybody knew the song
'Nellie the Elephant'
But Adidas, Kappa, Nike, pop songs,
that's all anybody thinks of now
I have lost all my colour
I was bright pink
now I'm white
She left me on the dusty shelf
with the sun in my eyes
All day, every day, bored, bored, bored
All she thinks about now is dolphins and fashion
You can't even see me
I'm hidden behind dolphins, bears etc
I used to get cuddled
played with, taken everywhere
Now I'm just left to fade away.

Alice Neve (11)
Upper Avon School

THE FAT TREE

I saw a tree
that was big and fat
I went over to see it
it had no leaves
they were all over the floor
the season was winter.
In the spring I went back
then it had some buds on it.
In the summer it had leaves on it
I sat under it for shade.

Suzanne Jewell (12)
Upper Avon School

THE OAK TREE

I see an oak tree
It gets bigger and bigger every day
It's dark and lumpy and bumpy with holes
I've got a tree house up there
It sits all day long
It's a bit like a camel's back.

Philip Emm (12)
Upper Avon School

SEASIDE

S ilvery sea clashing against the rocks
E very wave makes your back tingle
A boat's engine turning on makes you think about getting in the sea
   and swimming to the boat
S mells of fish and chips makes your mouth water
I 'd love to be eating fish and chips now
D eep blue sea feels really cold when you get in
E verybody's eating except you and it makes you really hungry.

Russell Hall (13)
Upper Avon School

TREES

The bark is so rough and bumpy like a sheet of sandpaper.
The twigs so thin and twisty like a corkscrew.
The trunk so tough and solid like a bulldozer with the brakes on.
The leaves so dark and crusty in the autumn wind.
The birds nesting in the summer sun from
when they were young.

Craig Stevens (13)
Upper Avon School

BOURNEMOUTH BEACH

Squawking seagulls flying around
Looking for crumbs on the ground.

Smash and crash of the waves
The rattling of people's roller-blades.

The sand is coloured different golds
Sweaty armpits smell of mould.

The sea is glistening silver and green
Someone drowning causes a scene.

The delicious smell of greasy fish and chips
Makes me smile and lick my lips.

The sun is shining bright and hot
Burning people smell of coconut sun block.

Dean Weeks (14)
Upper Avon School

A TREE RECYCLING

A tree is living
It provides us by giving, wonderful things like
Fruit, nuts, shelter in different seasons.
In the winter the trees are bare,
In the summer we get the glare of beautiful sunshine
But the trees protect us from the bright sunlight.

In the autumn the trees change colour
from green to red to brown.
In the spring, the tree starts its living cycle again.

Kirstin Imrie (12)
Upper Avon School

TREE POEM

A tree in a field
thin as a pencil.
The bark on the tree
crispy and rough,
the branches
thin, like an old person's hand.
The leaves are like veins
and move like water.
The tree stands out and opens
like a flower
and moves
like a snake.

Martin Winters (12)
Upper Avon School

AN AUTUMN TREE

The sky is dull
The leaves are falling
The people are cold
The leaves are soft

Branches are thick and
Look like an old person's arm

The trunk is wrinkled like an old face
With lumps and bumps

The roots look like old people's feet
And feel very cold like ice.

Gemma Brittain (12)
Upper Avon School

MY TREE

I look out of my window
and see a tree
tall, with great big branches
like skinny arms
coming to pick me up.
But then there's the leaves,
they're like thick fingers
with veins like old people's hands.
But then it comes to time,
I think where has it come from?
I don't know.
Its beauty just stands there
For all to admire it.

Kayleigh Smith (12)
Upper Avon School

TREES

Trees live in the woods, along with all the bugs,
Trees have branches as sharp as nails, because they scratch
against the rails,
Trees are tall, even if they lean against the wall,
In the summer the trees bloom, like a very colourful broom,
In the winter, trees get covered in snow, because it makes them glow,
Trees are the colour brown, because they never frown,
Some trees are smooth some are rough, but all trees are tough.
Some trees have bats, and some are surrounded by rats.

Andrew Milligan (13)
Upper Avon School

TREES

Trees trees in the summer
your leaves are green
Trees trees in the summer
children play on your branches
Trees trees in the summer
you stand tall and green

Trees trees in the autumn
your leaves float to the ground
Trees trees in the autumn
people say you look ugly but soon your leaves will be back
Trees trees in the autumn
you stand tall and brown

Trees trees in winter
all your leaves are gone
Trees trees in the winter your branches are brown and bare
Trees trees in the winter
you stand tall and sad

Trees trees in the spring
your leaves are coming back
Trees trees in the spring
your trunk is strong ready for summer
Trees trees in the spring you stand tall and happy.

Amy Cuthbertson (13)
Upper Avon School

SUMMER AT THE SEASIDE

Out of the car on the sand.
The sand is as hot as the sun and burns your feet.
In I go with a splash.
I feel like a cube of ice.
Slimy weed going down my legs.
Out I go and see wobbly jellyfish washed to the shore.

Down I go in the sand.
Burning my skin until it melts.
Up I go to the fairground.
Squawking seagulls crying like babies.
The air smelling as sweet as candyfloss.

Down I go to the shop.
Smelling the chips makes me hungry.
Seagulls coming down demanding food.

Down I go in the sand.
Sun burning in my eyes.
Silver sea glossy as glass.
Fluffy clouds sweet as candyfloss.

People walking as wet as fish.
Wetting you as they pass.
Come on then we're off.
Back to the car I jump in.
Dad says come on we're going home.

Pauline Collins (13)
Upper Avon School

BRAVE TREE

Standing tall and brave in the deep mid-winter,
Shaking with cold and bony fingers.
My branches full of snow.
My leaves used to be so green and lush
In the summer.
My dream for spring to return
And my roots to grow and my branches
To burst with life.

My friends the birds will once again nest in me.
Oh I will believe, I will be green again,
Full of colour and buds, feeling alive
Not brown and dull
Like a wrinkled old man's skin with
Bony fingers and prickly leaves,
My roots gnarled and twisted.
I wait patiently for my life to begin again,
As an oak tree.

Ferenc Magyar (13)
Upper Avon School